THE
BOOK OF HORSES

BOOKS BY FRED URQUHART

Novels

TIME WILL KNIT
THE FERRET WAS ABRAHAM'S DAUGHTER
JEZEBEL'S DUST
PALACE OF GREEN DAYS

Short Story Collections

I FELL FOR A SAILOR
THE CLOUDS ARE BIG WITH MERCY
SELECTED STORIES
THE LAST G.I. BRIDE WORE TARTAN
THE YEAR OF THE SHORT CORN
THE LAST SISTER
THE LAUNDRY GIRL AND THE POLE
PROUD LADY IN A CAGE
A DIVER IN CHINA SEAS
COLLECTED STORIES 1: THE DYING STALLION
COLLECTED STORIES 2: THE PLOUGHING MATCH

Books edited by Fred Urquhart

MODERN SCOTTISH SHORT STORIES (with Giles Gordon)
NO SCOTTISH TWILIGHT (with Maurice Lindsay)
SCOTTISH SHORT STORIES
W.S.C.: A CARTOON BIOGRAPHY OF WINSTON CHURCHILL
GREAT TRUE WAR ADVENTURES
MEN AT WAR
GREAT TRUE ESCAPE STORIES
THE CASSELL MISCELLANY 1848–1958
EVERYMAN'S DICTIONARY OF FICTIONAL CHARACTERS (with William Freeman)

THE
BOOK OF HORSES

edited by

F RED U RQUHART

WILLIAM MORROW AND COMPANY, INC.

NEW YORK 1981

Library of Congress Catalog Card Number: 81–82551
ISBN: 0–688–00419–9

First Edition
1 2 3 4 5 6 7 8 9 10

Typeset by CCC, printed and bound
in Great Britain by William Clowes (Beccles) Limited,
Beccles and London

TO

Catherine and Arthur Hayes

Contents

1

Ride a Cock-Horse

Ride a cock-horse to Banbury Cross,
To see a fine lady upon a white horse;
Rings on her fingers and bells on her toes,
And she shall have music wherever she goes.

Traditional

The Runaway

Robert Frost

Once when the snow of the year was beginning to fall,
We stopped by a mountain pasture to say, "Whose colt?"
A little Morgan had one forefoot on the wall,
The other curled at his breast. He dipped his head
And snorted at us. And then he had to bolt.
We heard the miniature thunder where he fled,
And we saw him, or thought we saw him, dim and gray,

Mother and Son, H. W. B. Davis

Like a shadow against the curtain of falling flakes.
"I think the little fellow's afraid of the snow.
He isn't winter-broken. It isn't play
With the little fellow at all. He's running away.
I doubt if even his mother could tell him, 'Sakes,
It's only weather.' He'd think she didn't know!
Where is his mother? He can't be out alone."
And now he comes again with clatter of stone,
And mounts the wall again with whited eyes
And all his tail that isn't hair up straight.
He shudders his coat as if to throw off flies.
"Whoever it is that leaves him out so late,
When other creatures have gone to stall and bin,
Ought to be told to come and take him in."

FROM

Lavengro

George Borrow

And it came to pass that, as I was standing by the door of the barrack stable, one of the grooms came out to me, saying, "I say, young gentleman, I wish you would give the cob a breathing this fine morning."

"Why do you wish me to mount him?" said I. "You know he is dangerous. I saw him fling you off his back a few days ago."

"Why, that's the very thing, master. I'd rather see anybody on his back than myself. He does not like me; but, to them he does, he can be as gentle as a lamb."

"But suppose," said I, "that he should not like me?"

"We shall soon see that, master," said the groom; "and, if so be he shows temper, I will be the first to tell you to get down. But there's no fear of that. You have never angered or insulted him, and to such as you, I say again, he'll be as gentle as a lamb."

"And how came you to insult him," said I, "knowing his temper as you do?"

"Merely through forgetfulness, master. I was riding him about a month ago, and having a stick in my hand, I struck him, thinking I was on another horse, or rather thinking of nothing at all. He has never forgiven me, though before that time he was the only friend I had in the world. I should like to see you on him, master."

A Horseman in a Wood, Jean-Baptiste Corot

"I should soon be off him. I can't ride."

"Then you are all right, master. There's no fear. Trust him for not hurting a young gentleman, an officer's son, who can't ride. If you were a blackguard dragoon, indeed, with long spurs, 'twere another thing. As it is, he'll treat you as if he were the elder brother that loves you. Ride! He'll soon teach you to ride, if you leave the matter with him. He's the best riding master in all Ireland, and the gentlest."

The cob was led forth. What a tremendous creature! I had frequently seen him before, and wondered at him. He was barely fifteen hands, but he had the girth of a metropolitan dray-horse.

Man on a Cob (St George), Fernando Botero

His head was small in comparison with his immense neck, which curved down nobly to his wide back. His chest was broad and fine, and his shoulders models of symmetry and strength. He stood well and powerfully upon his legs, which were somewhat short. In a word, he was a gallant specimen of the genuine Irish cob, a species at one time not uncommon, but at the present day nearly extinct.

"There!" said the groom, as he looked at him, half-admiringly, half sorrowfully, "with sixteen stone on his back, he'll trot fourteen miles in an hour; with your nine stone, some two and a half more, ay, and clear a six-foot wall at the end of it."

"I'm half afraid," said I. "I had rather you would ride him."

"I'd rather so, too, if he would let me; but he remembers the blow. Now, don't be afraid, young master, he's longing to go out himself. He's been trampling with his feet these three days, and I know what that means. He'll let anybody ride him but myself, and thank them; but to me he says, 'No! you struck me.'"

"But," said I, "where's the saddle?"

"Never mind the saddle; if you are ever to be a frank rider, you must begin without a saddle. Besides, if he felt a saddle, he would think you don't trust him, and leave you to yourself. Now, before you mount, make his acquaintance. See there, how he kisses you and licks your face, and see how he lifts his foot; that's to shake hands. You may trust him. Now you are on his back at last; mind how you hold the bridle—gently, gently! It's not four pair of hands like yours can hold him if he wishes to be off. Mind what I tell you—leave it all to him."

Off went the cob at a slow and gentle trot, too fast, however, for so inexperienced a rider. I soon felt myself sliding off. The animal perceived it too, and instantly stood stone still till I had righted myself; and now the groom came up. "When you feel yourself going," said he, "don't lay hold of the mane, that's no use; mane never yet saved man from falling, no more than straw from drowning; it's his sides you must cling to with your calves and feet, till you learn to balance yourself. That's it; now abroad with you. I'll bet my comrade a pot of beer that you'll be a regular rough rider by the time you come back."

And so it proved. I followed the directions of the groom, and the cob gave me every assistance. How easy is riding, after the first timidity is got over, to supple and youthful limbs; and there is no second fear. The creature soon found that the nerves of his rider were in proper tone. Turning his head half round, he made a kind of whining noise, flung out a little foam, and set off.

In less than two hours I had made the circuit of the Devil's Mountain, and was returning along the road, bathed in perspiration, but screaming with delight; the cob laughing in his equine way, scattering foam and pebbles to the left and right, and trotting at the rate of sixteen miles an hour.

Oh, that ride! that first ride!—most truly it was an epoch in my existence; and I still look back to it with feelings of longing and regret. People may talk of first love—it is a very agreeable event, I dare say— but give me the flush, and triumph, and glorious sweat of a first ride, like mine on the mighty cob! My whole frame was shaken, it is true; and during one long week I could hardly move foot or hand, but what of that? By that one trial I had become free, as I may say, of the whole equine species. No more fatigue, no more stiffness of joints, after that first ride round the Devil's Hill on the cob.

Oh, that cob! that Irish cob!—may the sod lie lightly over the bones of the strongest, speediest, and most gallant of its kind! Oh, the days when, issuing from the barrack-gate of Templemore, we commenced our hurry-skurry just as inclination led—now across the fields—direct over stone walls and running brooks—mere pastime for the cob!—sometimes along the road to Thurles and Holy Cross, even to distant Cahir!—what was distance to the cob?

[7]

It was thus that the passion for the equine race was first awakened within me—a passion which, up to the present time, has been rather on the increase than diminishing. It is no blind passion; the horse being a noble and generous creature, intended by the All-Wise to be the helper and friend of man, to whom he stands next in the order of creation. On many occasions of my life I have been much indebted to the horse, and have found in him a friend and coadjutor, when human help and sympathy were not to be obtained. It is therefore natural enough that I should love the horse; but the love which I entertain for him has always been blended with respect; for I soon perceived that, though disposed to be the friend and helper of man, he is by no means inclined to be his slave; in which respect he differs from the dog, who will crouch when beaten; whereas the horse spurns, for he is aware of his own worth, and that he carries death within the horn of his heel. If, therefore, I found it easy to love the horse, I found it equally natural to respect him.

FROM

The Red Pony

John Steinbeck

Jody never waited for the triangle to get him out of bed after the coming of the pony. It became his habit to creep out of bed even before his mother was awake, to slip into his clothes and to go quietly down to the barn to see Gabilan. In the gray quiet mornings when the land and the brush and the houses and the trees were silver-gray and black like a photograph negative, he stole toward the barn, past the sleeping stones and the sleeping cypress tree. The turkeys, roosting in the tree out of coyotes' reach, clicked drowsily. The fields glowed with a gray frost-like light and in the dew the tracks of rabbits and of fieldmice stood out sharply. The good dogs came stiffly out of their little houses, hackles up and deep growls in their throats. Then they caught Jody's scent, and their stiff tails rose up and waved a greeting—Doubletree Mutt with the big thick tail, and Smasher, the incipient shepherd—then went lazily back to their warm beds.

It was a strange time and a mysterious journey, to Jody—an extension of a dream. When he first had the pony he liked to torture himself during the trip by thinking Gabilan would not be in his stall, and worse, would never have been there. And he had other delicious little self-induced pains. He thought how the rats had gnawed ragged holes in the red saddle, and how the mice had nibbled Gabilan's tail until it was stringy and thin. He usually ran the last little way to the barn. He unlatched the rusty hasp of the barn door and stepped in, and, no matter how quietly he opened the door, Gabilan was always looking at him over the barrier of the box stall and Gabilan

A Boy Holding a Horse, Aelbert Cuyp

whinnied softly and stamped his front foot, and his eyes had big sparks of red fire in them like oakwood embers.

Sometimes, if the work-horses were to be used that day, Jody found Billy Buck in the barn harnessing and currying. Billy stood with him and looked long at Gabilan and he told Jody a great many things about horses. He explained that they were terribly afraid for their feet, so that

Pumpkin with a Stable Lad, George Stubbs

one must make a practice of lifting the legs and patting the hooves and ankles to remove their terror. He told Jody how horses love conversation. He must talk to the pony all the time, and tell him the reasons for everything. Billy wasn't sure a horse could understand everything that was said to him, but it was impossible to say how much was understood. A horse never kicked up a fuss if someone he liked explained things to him. Billy could give examples, too. He had known, for instance, a horse nearly dead-beat with fatigue to perk up when told it was only a little farther to his destination. And he had known a horse paralysed with fright to come out of it when his rider told him what it was that was frightening him. While he talked in the mornings, Billy Buck cut twenty or thirty straws into neat three-inch lengths and struck them into his hat-band. Then, during the whole day, if he wanted to pick his teeth or merely to chew on something, he had only to reach up for one of them.

Jody listened carefully, for he knew and the whole country knew that Billy Buck was a fine hand with horses. Billy's own horse was a stringy cayuse with a hammer head, but he nearly always won the first prizes at the stock trials. Billy could rope a steer, take a double half-hitch about the horn with his riata, and dismount, and his horse would play the steer as an angler plays a fish, keeping a tight rope until the steer was down or beaten.

Every morning, after Jody had curried and brushed the pony, he let down the barrier of the stall, and Gabilan thrust past him and raced down the barn and into the corral. Around and around he galloped, and sometimes he jumped forward and landed on stiff legs. He stood quivering, stiff ears forward, eyes rolling so that the whites showed, pretending to be frightened. At last he walked snorting to the water-trough and buried his nose in the water up to the nostrils. Jody was proud then, for he knew that was the way to judge a horse. Poor horses only touched their lips to the water, but a fine spirited beast put his whole nose and mouth under, and only left room to breathe.

Then Jody stood and watched the pony, and he saw things he had never noticed about any other horse, the sleek, sliding flank muscles and the cords of the buttocks, which flexed like a closing fist, and the shine the sun put on the red coat. Having seen horses all his life, Jody had never looked at them very closely before. But now he noticed the moving ears which gave expression and even inflection of expression to the face. The pony talked with his ears. You could tell exactly how he felt about everything by the way his ears pointed. Sometimes they were stiff and upright and sometimes lax and sagging. They went back when he was angry or fearful, and forward when he was anxious and curious and pleased; and their exact position indicated which emotion he had.

Billy Buck kept his word. In the early fall the training began. First there was the halter-breaking, and that was the hardest because it was the first thing. Jody held a carrot and coaxed and promised and pulled on the rope. The pony set his feet like a burro when he felt the strain. But before long he learned. Jody walked all over the ranch leading him. Gradually he took to dropping the rope until the pony followed him unled wherever he went.

And then came the training on the long halter. That was slower work. Jody stood in the middle of the circle, holding the long halter. He clucked with his tongue and the pony started to walk in a big circle, held in by the long rope. He clucked again to make the pony trot, and again to make him gallop. Around and around Gabilan went thundering and enjoying it immensely. Then he called "Whoa," and the pony stopped. It was not long until Gabilan was perfect at it. But in many ways he was a bad pony. He bit Jody in the legs and stomped on Jody's feet. Now and then his ears went back and he aimed a tremendous kick at the boy. Every time he did one of these bad things, Gabilan settled back and seemed to laugh at himself.

The Mare's Head

Alexei Tolstoy

Once upon a time there lived an old man and an old woman. They had two daughters. The old man had a daughter and the old woman had a daughter.

The old woman took a dislike to her stepdaughter and she said to her husband:

"Take her away, wherever you like."

There was no help for it. So the peasant drove his daughter into the forest. There he saw a little hut, with nobody in it, so he took his daughter inside and said:

"You stay here and I will go and chop some wood."

When she was inside he fastened the branch of a birch tree to the door, and as the wind blew, the branch tapped on the door and the girl thought that her father was chopping wood. But her father had gone home long since.

Whether the time was long or short, no one knows, but out of the forest came a mare's head with no legs and no tail, went to the hut and said:

"Little girl, little girl, open the gate for me."

The girl ran out and opened the gate.

The mare's head entered the hut and said:

"Little girl, little girl, lift me from the threshold on to the bench."

The girl took it up and lifted it from the threshold on to the bench. Then the mare's head said:

"Little girl, little girl, make the bed for me and put me to bed."

The girl made the bed and put the mare's head into it, and the mare's head said to her:

"Climb into my right ear and out of my left ear."

So the girl got into its right ear and came out through its left ear and at once became very beautiful indeed. Then a carriage with horses stopped before the little hut and the little girl was taken back to her father's house.

Everybody was amazed. The girl gave presents to them all, to her father, the old woman and the old woman's daughter.

Then the old woman said to her husband:

"Take my daughter where you took yours."

The peasant did not say no. He drove the old woman's daughter to the little hut in the forest. He took her in and said:

"You stay here while I go and chop wood."

And again he tied a branch of a birch tree to the door. It tapped against the door and the old woman's daughter thought:

"My stepfather is chopping wood."

Blood Horse, John Steading

Whether the time was long or short no one knows, but a mare's head without legs or tail came to the hut and said:

"Little girl, little girl, open the gate for me."

And the old woman's daughter answered it:

"You are not a lady, you can open it for yourself."

The mare's head entered the hut.

"Little girl, little girl, lift me up from the threshold, make the bed and put me to sleep on it."

And the old woman's daughter said to it:

"Even at home I do not make the bed and I am not going to begin to do it for you."

"Little girl, little girl," said the mare's head, "climb into my left ear and out of my right."

The old woman's daughter got into its left ear and came out through its right, not a beauty but a toothless old crone.

Translated from the Russian by Evgenia Schimanskaya

Shetland Pony

Maurice Lindsay

A loose fold of steam idling
slumped in a roll of wet grass:
bridle in hand, me, soothing, sidling
up to its rest. One move to pass

Shetland Pony

the loop round its passivity,
and eyes clench, nostrils itch,
its breath flaring activity
as hocks and neck bend in a twitch

that plucks it up to throw a lunging
proud parabola. It shakes
the field's roots, and leaves me plunging
blundered angles out. It makes

knots in the wide circumference
of centuries it darkly flings
around that less old arrogance
by which my domination clings;

then suddenly trundle-bellies in
from what it's proved to where I stand
haltered in sweat; and, duty done,
nuzzles confinement from my hand.

Coco

Guy de Maupassant

In all the country round the Lucas Farm was know as "the Hall". Nobody knew why; except that the country people no doubt associated an idea of opulence with the word, and this particular farm was certainly the largest, the best-kept, and the richest in the county.

It consisted of an immense enclosure, shut in by five lines of magnificent trees to protect the delicate, twisted apple-trees against the strong winds from the plains; a row of long tile-covered buildings for storing corn and fodder; a range of fine cattle-sheds built of flint; stables to hold thirty horses; and a red brick farmhouse, which looked like a small château.

The manure heaps were neat and orderly; there were kennels for the watch dogs, and innumerable fowl ran about in the long grass.

Every day, at dinner-time, fifteen persons, made up of the family, farm-hands and servants, sat down at the long kitchen table where the soup was steaming in a great earthenware tureen

Farming Scene, from manuscript of Virgil's *Georgics*

ornamented with blue flowers.

The animals—horses, cows, pigs and sheep—were fat, clean and well-cared for; and Farmer Lucas, a tall man inclining to stoutness, walked round his estate three times a day to see that everything was as it should be.

A very aged white horse was kept at the far end of the stable for sentimental reasons, his mistress wishing him to be kept in comfort till the end of his days, because he had always been a favourite, and had many associations for her. A young scamp of fifteen, by name Isidore Duval, though he was always called Zidore for short, was paid to take charge of this decrepit animal. In winter he had to give him his measure of corn and see to his bedding, and in summer he had to go four times a day and move the stake to which he was tied, so that he should have plenty of fresh grass.

The poor old creature was nearly done for; his legs were swollen at the knee and fetlock, so that he moved with difficulty; while his coat, which no one now troubled to groom, hung on him like a shock of white hair, and a few long lashes gave an expression of unutterable sadness to his eyes.

When Zidore took him out to grass he had to pull hard on the halter, Coco moved so slowly; and the boy panted and swore as he tugged, furious at having to look after such an old crock.

The farm-hands soon noticed the urchin's hatred of Coco, and amused themselves by talking to him incessantly about his horse, in order to exasperate him. His comrades also teased him, and he became known in the village as Coco-Zidore.

The boy grew more and more furious, and began to plan how he could be revenged on the animal. He was a thin, scraggy youth, very dirty, with long legs and a mop of thick red hair which stood up stiffly on his head. He appeared somewhat feeble-minded and stammered when he spoke, as though ideas found it difficult to form themselves in his heavy brute-like brain.

He had never been able to understand why his mistress kept Coco, and he hated to see good food wasted on such a useless animal. It seemed to him an injustice that the horse should be fed a moment after he had ceased to work, and a shame to throw away good oats—and oats were so dear, too—on a paralytic old horse. Sometimes, even, despite the strict orders of Farmer Lucas, he would economize over the animal's rations, giving Coco only half a measure of oats instead of a whole and reducing his allowance of hay and straw. And a great hatred arose in his childish soul, the hatred of a grasping, sly, brutal, cowardly son of the soil.

As soon as summer came round, he had once more to go out to change the beast's pasture. It was some distance, and the anger in the boy's heart grew fiercer every day as he plodded heavily along through the cornfields. The men working on the land would amuse themselves by shouting after him:

"Hullo, Zidore, be sure you give my respects to Coco."

He made no reply; but he kept a whip hidden in the hedge and, as soon as he had moved the stake, and the old animal had begun to graze again, he would come up treacherously behind him and lash him across the hams. The animal would kick and rear, but all he could do to avoid the blows was to race round and round at the end of his tether, as though he were in a circus. And the boy ran behind him, beating the horse madly, his teeth clenched with anger.

Then he would go off slowly, without turning round, while the horse gazed at him out of his old eyes, with heaving flanks and quivering nostrils. Nor would he put his white-haired, bony old head to the ground again, until he had seen the boy's blue blouse disappear safely into the distance.

Now that the nights were warm, Coco was allowed to sleep out on the edge of the stream behind the wood. Zidore was the only person who went to see him. He sat a few yards from him, on the side of a slope, where he would stay for half-an-hour at a time, every now and then hurling a sharp stone at the animal, who stood upright, staring continuously at his enemy and not daring to put his head down to graze until he had departed.

One thought was always present in the urchin's mind: "Why go on feeding the animal now it does no work?" It seemed to him that the brute had the deliberate intention of consuming the food that rightfully belonged to others, until there would be nothing left for man or God, or for him, Zidore, either, who had to work for his living every day of the year.

So little by little he diminished the area of fresh grass which the horse was supposed to enjoy every day, by moving the picket to which he was tied to a smaller and smaller distance from its old position.

The beast grew thinner and feebler, and was plainly dying. Too weak to break his cord, he could only stretch his head towards the fine lush grass so close to him, the grass which he could see and smell, but not touch.

One morning Zidore had another idea. It was not to move Coco's picket at all. He had done enough tramping up and down to look after such a carcase.

But he continued to come, in order to enjoy the spectacle of his revenge. The animal looked at him anxiously; Zidore did not beat him that day, contenting himself with walking round him, with his hands in his pockets. He even made a pretence of changing Coco's position, but he only drove the picket deeper into the same hole, and took himself off, delighted with the new plan.

Seeing him departing, the horse whinnied to bring him back. But the boy broke into a run, and left him alone in the meadow, securely tied, and without a blade of grass within his reach.

The Frugal Meal, John Frederick Herring

Maddened by hunger, the animal struggled to reach the grass which touched the end of his nose. He fell on his knees, stretched his neck forward, and thrust out his thick, slobbering lips. But in vain. All day he wore his body out with frightful and unavailing struggles. And the hunger which devoured him was made all the more terrible by the green pastures by which he was surrounded.

The boy did not return again that day. He wandered off to the woods to look for birds'-nests.

He reappeared the following day. Coco was stretched at full length on the ground. He got up when he saw the boy, expecting to be given a change of pasture at last.

But Zidore did not even touch the mallet which lay ready on the grass. He walked up, looked at the animal, threw a handful of mud at his nose, which broke in splashes of black over his white skin, and departed whistling.

The horse remained standing while the boy could still be seen; then, knowing well that his efforts to reach the grass round him were useless, he lay down again on his side, and shut his eyes.

Next day Zidore did not appear at all.

When he came, the day after, Coco was still lying on the ground, and he realized that the animal was dead.

He stood a long time, contemplating his work with satisfaction, though at the same time a little startled that it was over so soon. He touched the corpse with his foot, lifted one of its legs and let it fall again, sat down on its side, and stayed there, his eyes fixed on the ground, thinking of nothing.

When he returned to the farm he did not say what had happened, because he wanted to go birds'-nesting again in the time when he would ordinarily have been moving the horse's tether.

He went to see it again the following day. Some crows flew away as he came up. Innumerable flies were walking over the body, and filling the air round it with their buzzing.

He announced the news, this time, on his return. The horse was so old that no one was in the least surprised. The farmer gave orders to two labourers:

"Take your spades, and dig a hole where he lies."

The men buried the horse on the very spot where he died of hunger.

A fine crop of rich grass sprang up, nourished by his poor old body.

Translated from the French by J. Lewis May

Waiting for Death, Thomas Bewick

2

Horse Working

Here, in this island, the work is almost all done by the horses. The horses plough the ground; they sow the ground; they hoe the ground; they carry the corn home; they thresh it out; and they carry it to market: nay, in this island they *rake* the ground; they rake up the straggling straws and ears; so that they do the whole, excepting the reaping and the mowing. It is impossible to have an idea of anything more miserable than the state of the labourers in this part of the country.

from Rural Rides *by William Cobbett*

St George and the Dragon, Paolo Uccello

detail from the *Bayeux Tapestry*

Horse

George Mackay Brown

The horse at the shore
Casks of red apples, skull, a barrel of rum

The horse in the field
Plough, ploughman, gulls, a furrow, a cornstalk

Ploughing on the Downs, Robert Bevan

The horse in the peatbog
Twelve baskets of dark fire

The horse at the pier
Letters, bread, paraffin, one passenger, papers

The horse at the show
Ribbons, raffia, high bright hooves

The horse in the meadow
A stallion, a russet gale, between two hills

The horse at the burn
Quenching a long flame in the throat

A Wagon and Team of Horses, Rosa Bonheur

Akenfield

Ronald Blythe

John Grout, aged 88 in 1968, began work on his father's farm in Suffolk at the age of eleven. In his teens he got a job with Lord Rendlesham. "He was a rare big gentleman in the neighbourhood and was famous for his horses. Why, he kept three men who did nothing else but see after the stallions. There were scores of horses—mostly shires and punches. The greatest of these was a punch stallion called Big Boy who had won so many brass medals he couldn't carry them all on his harness. Men came from all over to see these horses but they hardly ever saw Big Boy. He was hid up and not to be looked at.

The head horseman was called the 'lord'—and that's what he was, lord of all the horses. That was me one day, I was lord of the horses. The place ran like clockwork. All the harnessing was done in strict order, first this, then that. The ploughing teams left and returned to the stable yards according to the rank of the ploughman. If you happened to get back before someone senior to you, you just had to wait in the lane until he had arrived. *Then* you could go, but not before.

The horses were friends and loved like men. Some men would do more for a horse than they would for a wife. The ploughmen talked softly to their teams all day long and you could see the horses listening. Although the teams ploughed twenty yards apart, the men didn't talk much to each other, except sometimes they sang. Each man ploughed in his own fashion and with his own mark. It looked all the same if you didn't know about ploughing, but a farmer could walk on a field ploughed by ten different teams and tell which bit was ploughed by which. Sometimes he would pay a penny an acre extra for perfect ploughing. Or he would make a deal with the ploughman—'free rent for good work.' That could mean £5 a year. The men worked perfectly to get this, but they also worked perfectly because it was *their* work. It belonged to them. It was theirs.

The plough-teams left for the field at seven sharp in the morning and finished at three in the afternoon. They reckoned a ploughman would walk eleven miles a day on average. It wasn't hard walking in the dirt, not like the rough roads. The horsemen were the big men on the farm. They kept in with each other and had secrets. They were a whispering lot. If someone who wasn't a ploughman came upon them and they happened to be talking, they'd soon change the conversation! And if you discovered them in a room where the horse medicine was, it was covered up double quick. They made the horses obey with a sniff from a rag which they kept in their pockets. Caraway seeds had something to do with it, I believe, though others say different.

A lot of farmers hid their horses during the Great War, when the officers came round. The officers always gave good money for a horse, but sometimes the horses were like brothers and the men couldn't let them go, so they hid them."

A Cotswold Farm, Gilbert Spencer

Quarter Horses

Pers Crowell

"He's a sleepy little hoss that can unwind like lightnin'!" That is the Texan's laconic description of the Quarter Horse. Tremendous speed and even temperament are the factors that make this little animal valuable to those who need a "using" horse. From the standpoint of utility, no horse can lay greater claim to his right of being.

The Quarter Horse has always been found at the outermost fringe of the frontiers of America because he could be counted upon when the jobs were difficult.

For those who think that the Quarter-type horse is a "Johnny-come-lately", let us leave the great cow country of the Southwest and go back about three hundred years to the time of the early English colonists in Virginia and the Carolinas.

As early as 1611, Sir Thomas Dale brought seventeen horses from England. Other stock was undoubtedly brought into the English colonies from the Indian and Spanish settlements to the south, and even before there was sufficient timber cut from the land to form an oval race track, "short" horses were burning up the forest paths with their bursts of terrific speed. By 1656, quarter-mile races were popular, and in 1690, short races with substantial purses were offered for Colonial quarter-of-a-mile race horses.

It is interesting to picture the difficult living conditions of those times. It had only been eighty-four years since King James I had given to the Virginia Company, under the Royal charter of 1606, a map of the territory which included a 75- to 100-mile strip extending along the Atlantic seaboard from what is now the southern boundary of South Carolina to the Canadian border. So wild and impenetrable was this strip that it was believed the great Western ocean lay to its west. The task of hewing a livelihood out of such country was laborious and dangerous. The horses which served the colonists had to be of tough fiber and able to perform the most difficult equine tasks. It would be another eighty-five years before Daniel Boone would be able to thrust open the old Wilderness Trail in Kentucky.

Perhaps many of the racecourses over which Colonial Quarter Horses ran were the old war trails of the Indians who, in the tragic year of 1622, had massacred at least one-third of the English settlers in Virginia. It is easy to imagine the reckless abandon with which the early Cavaliers grasped at, in fleeting moments, such sportive equine diversion.

"Where did these horses get their stamina," we may ask, "and where did they originally come from?"

The origin of the early horses along the Atlantic seaboard has never been fully established, but parts of the puzzle can be put together. There is much evidence to support the contention of Quarter Horse breeders and enthusiasts that this little horse is the oldest fixed type in America today. Let us consider some of the possible sources in the century before the English colonists started racing their Quarter Horses.

There is little doubt that the first horses to place a hoof on American soil in any number were the sixteen landed by Cortez in preparation for his conquests in Mexico. These horses—eleven stallions and five mares—were put ashore in the year 1519. They were of Spanish variety, two of them being of the famous Jennet breed. It is possible, but highly improbable, that of the horses that strayed and multiplied, one could have migrated to the eastern part of the continent in the one-hundred-year period before the landing of the first English colonists.

On August 1, 1539, De Soto and his party started northward from Florida with 200 horses. On this expedition he spent considerable time in the land of the Chickasaw Indians. When he was ready to depart from this section, he demanded native male carriers and women. This the Chickasaws considered an insult, and they fell upon the Spaniards at dawn. By the time those in the town were aware of what was happening, half the houses were in flames. The confusion that followed left the soldiers no time to arm or saddle their mounts. The terrorized horses snapped their halters and stampeded, a few being lost in the fire. This encounter would have been complete victory for the Chickasaws and would have put an end to the expedition if the Indians had not mistakenly believed the sound of running horses to mean that the cavalry had managed to mount and pursue them.

Wild Horses at Play, George Catlin

It is possible to believe that some of the horses that stampeded that March morning, remained at liberty until the Chickasaws later captured them. Perhaps these were the horses which the Chickasaw Indians are reported to have obtained from the Spanish settlers. Chickasaw horses were raced at quarter-mile distances, but aside from their more glamorous holiday-sports use, the animals were good at plain labor and for purposes of transportation. Writers of those times referred to the Chickasaw as a breed, and their descriptions give an excellent picture of the horse. He was small from the standpoint of height, averaging around 13 hands 2 inches; he was closely coupled and well muscled. At short distances, he showed great speed but was not noted for endurance in long races. It was conceded that the Chickasaw horse was the best all-round utility horse in Colonial America.

The Horse in the Furrow

George Ewart Evans

In 1797 when Arthur Young was urging Suffolk horse-breeders to a new policy, the Government in a panic burst of taxation to meet the cost of the war, placed a tax on all horses. The relevant parts of the Statute are:

Schedule C: A Schedule of Rates and Duties payable for all *Horses, Mares* and *Geldings* kept and used by any Person or Persons for the Purpose of riding or for the Purpose of drawing any Carriage chargeable with Duty by this Act—

For one such Horse, Mare or Gelding and no more and so on to:	£1 4s. od.
For twenty such Horses, Mares or Geldings or upwards	£2 15s. od.

Schedule D: A Schedule of the Rates and Duties payable for Horses, Mares and Geldings, not charged with any Duty, according to Schedule C and also Mules:

For each Horse, Mare or Gelding kept by any Person and not charged with any Duty	6s. od.

It may, or may not, be some consolation to farmers to know that their ancestors a century and a half ago were not spared the necessity of wrestling with schedules. . . .

The purpose of the tax, apart from the revenue accruing from it, may have been to divert as many horses as possible from civilian to military service, but the effect on the farmer or landowner interested enough to breed horses and to attempt to improve his stock must have been disastrous. For however real a farmer's enthusiasm for improving the breed, it could not be unimpaired by the insult to his pocket and the rebuff to his public spirit that the tax seemed to offer.

The state of development of the Suffolk horse up to this time was briefly as follows. At first he was "a very plain made horse", to use an euphemism of the time; and even the most partisan advocates of the old breed had to admit he was no oil-painting. But his looks belied his true qualities, and during his hey-day looks, in any case, were not at a premium; for competition was not by parade or exhibition in the show ring but by actual proof of a horse's strength in drawing heavy loads of sand or stones. In this, the low position of the old Suffolker's shoulders gave him a tremendous advantage. Yet during the next forty years, in spite of the war and the discouragement of the horse-tax, the breed was so improved as to become one of the finest in the country. A Suffolk took the prize for "the best horse for agricultural purposes" at the first meeting of the newly formed Royal Agricultural Society of England at Oxford in 1839. . . .

What are the main characteristics of the Suffolk breed of horse? The first and obvious one is the clearly defined colour. The colour of the old breed was distinguished by the now obsolete term sorrel—a name which still remains in many Suffolk inns. The colour today is chestnut; but there are seven shades of chestnut, the red, the golden, the lemon or yellow, the light, mealy chestnut, the dark, the dull-dark, and lastly the bright chestnut. The bright chestnut is considered the most characteristic colour and, all other things being equal, the one to be preferred.

The Suffolk's head is big with a broad forehead, and often with a star on it or a *shim* or *blaze* down the face; the neck deep in the collar and tapering to a graceful setting of the head; the shoulders long and muscular and thrown well back at the withers. The wellrounded rib—the barrel chest that has helped to give the Suffolk the name of Punch—is a distinctive feature, as is the deep carcase. This last is one of the first essentials of a true Suffolk; for it was bred for use on the farm, and for use on the Suffolk farms in particular, where it was the custom for the horses to work a long day from 6.30 a.m. to 2.30 p.m. without nosebag or any break for rations. An ample *bread-basket* was thus indispensable to the Suffolk; and this characteristic—emphasised by selective breeding—is another example of the inspired fusion of breed, local custom and use that has gained East Anglian farmers such a deserved reputation as stockraisers.

The shapely outline of back loin and quarters is as noticeable as the deep carcase. "Feet, joints and legs—the legs should be straight with fair, sloping pasterns, big knees and long clean hocks on short cannon bones, free from coarse hair; the feet should have plenty of size with circular form protecting the frog; walk, smart and true; trot—well balanced all round with good action. If one were asked the question, what are the four chief characteristics of the Suffolk Horse? the answer would certainly be—colour, quality, compactness and hardy constitution."

The Suffolk Punch

Bent's Fort

David Lavender

The Cheyennes had been a timid, earthbound folk, living precariously in the lake country of northern Minnesota. Terrible pressures were on them. It was the time of the great displacements caused by the advance of the white men. The uprooted tribes of eastern Canada and the eastern United States, edging westward, warred furiously among themselves and with their farther neighbors in a contest not only for living room but also for the right to carry on into the wilderness, at a middleman's profit, the trade goods arriving from Hudson Bay and across the Great Lakes. Chippewas pressed against the Cheyennes; Sioux pressed them; Crees and Assiniboins harried them. Some of these tribes, living nearer white men, possessed guns. The Cheyennes did not, and the unequal odds forced them slowly southwestward across the Red River of the North and on to the Missouri. In time, of course, the seepage of trade brought them guns. . . . Though few of the Cheyennes had yet seen a white man, they were already becoming dependent on his goods. Who now can estimate the labor saved by so simple a thing as an iron awl, or by a kettle for boiling water in place of the old-fashioned buffalo paunch into which hot stones were dropped? How gauge the freedom of spirit that sprang from the ability to strike fire with flint rather than depend on twirling sticks or on precious coals apprehensively carried in a smoldering buffalo chip?

Despite the primitive agriculture they had learned, life remained precarious. Sometimes they caught antelope in pits or attacked buffalo floundering in deep snow. On other rare occasions footmen, ceremoniously painted with red earth, were able to slay buffalo by driving them over steep bluffs. Magic was important—the proper waving of eagle feathers, of circular willow wands. If the charm was right, a herd could be harassed into brush pens behind whose flimsy walls guards waving blankets got the beasts milling and thus approachable for slaughter. Such lucky chances were bright spots in a life of semi-starvation, an opportunity to dry jerky, to pound desiccated slabs of flesh into a powder, mix it with crushed berries, and seal it with melted fat against the future. But normal days were filled with grubbing up roots, gathering the eggs of shore birds, hunting out the burrows of badgers and skunks.

A foot people, they could carry little until they learned to domesticate dogs: they were of use in sounding alarms, keeping the grounds clear of refuse, and furnishing emergency rations during times of need. After a while someone else had the notion of putting packs on them, and then of attaching travois—practices that continued into historic times. A squaw might have as many as a dozen canines on which she packed small articles and to which she hitched diminutive travois, runaways being prevented by leashes. In olden days, patriarchs said, the dogs were bigger than the ones white men saw—inevitable degeneration!—yet bulky transport was beyond them. Although precious buffalo hides were now being used for shelter, not many could be dog-packed from place to place. As a result lodges remained mere hutches of bent willows over which the coverings were draped.

And then, somewhere near the Black Hills, the whole economy changed. The Cheyennes met the horse.

The animals came to the Plains Indians by trade with or theft from the Spanish settlements of Texas and New Mexico. By trade and theft they continued northward, tribe to tribe, until by the third quarter of the eighteenth century they had reached Canada. Along the way they became as complete a symbol of well-being as any that a people has ever worshiped. Valuable of themselves, they could purchase whatever a man desired; but in larger measure they were an expression not merely of possession but of the heart's greatest joys, its most profound yearnings. When a young man wooed, his bringing horses to the lodge of his sweetheart's father was more than just a bribe. When husband and wife planned on a child, they often sent about the village crier to make public announcement of the happiness—and then distributed horses. When a man child was named or when a boy grew doughty enough to kill his first buffalo calf; when a girl passed through her first menstrual period and so achieved significance as the potential mother of warriors, the proud parents held feasts—and gave away horses. A warrior's outstanding feat

Pawnee Catching Wild Horses, George Catlin

[32]

Jumped, Charles M. Russell

might be signalized by his taking a new name—and passing around horses. When he died his favorite mount was slain with him. Should he break one of the few tribal rules of which village society as a whole took cognizance (such as violating the plans for a communal hunt), the supreme punishment was the killing of his horses.

This cultural dominance was but the pomp attendant on economic dominance. By bringing buffalo regularly within reach of arrow and lance, the horse made food surpluses possible for the first time. Life achieved a nobility above mere subsistence. Not the least of man's dignities lies in the shelter he occupies, and now a mounted warrior could provide ample material for one of the most functional dwellings ever devised, the mobile tepee of the Plains Indians. For the sake of their homes, savage women learned to tan buffalo hides and thus developed, by chance, a trade article that would bring the commerce of the whites sweeping over the prairies. That the commerce in time would mean extinction was, naturally enough, not recognized, its immediate luxuries being too dazzling to question.

[33]

A Horse

Alan Bold

Bred to bear a burden,
Tolerated so he might lift
Examples of humanity from the ground
He is sleek, strong, supple, stoic, swift.

He might achieve transient fame
By winning, with their help, a famous race;
He might win money for the punters,
Be photographed beside a famous face.

He might end up being shot
Out of human sympathy;
Being wept over by purveyors
Of horsy empathy.

Though magnificent he is not admired
For his gait or his gloss
Or his arrogant elegance
But for what he does.

Someday some of the people will let
The horse be a horse;
Not a carrier like this one's ancestor
Who walked men through wars.

Study of a Horse, Jacques Callot

3

Horse Talking

I speak Spanish to God, Italian to women, French to men, and German to my horse.

Emperor Charles V (1500–58)

Mares and Foals in a Landscape, George Stubbs

George IV's Persian Horses Being Taken Out for Exercise, H. B. Chalon

Adam Bede

George Eliot

"Bless me! how the brook has overflowed. Suppose we have a canter, now we're at the bottom of the hill."

That is the great advantage of dialogue on horseback; it can be merged any minute into a trot or canter, and one might have escaped from Socrates himself in the saddle.

A Morning Ride in the Bois de Boulogne, Auguste Renoir

Chariot Race in Roman Circus

FROM

Travel Light

Naomi Mitchison

Halla knew her way to the racing stables by the Hippodrome (in Byzantium). She had talked to any intelligent-looking horses while she was in the city, and also on the days when the men had gone out and left her at home, to the kites which came down on to the roof and were more knowing than the birds of the deep forest, but smelt worse. The ones that knew their way best about Micklegard were the rats, all the same. They enjoyed the city, more perhaps than most of the men and women in it, and they knew all the little paths about it, on all levels from drains to roof-tops. Especially they knew their way to all the stables, and how to get at the corn. Halla never threw stones at the rats. They were no worse than others. She said this to the men, who saw in it a sign from God to whom all life is blessed. But they threw stones all the same. The rats never came into the room when the men were there unless they were asleep. But they knew Halla. They knew Halla as friendly to rats. When she asked them a way they told her or showed her. Why not?

The racing stables were big yards with stalls off them; the grooms slept with the horses. The charioteers, who were mostly little men with quick tempers, lived in the upper rooms. They quarrelled and sulked and sometimes poisoned one another out of jealousy. If this was found out, the one who had done it had his head held down on the shoeing anvil and his brains knocked out with a hammer; they were mostly slaves. But they went on doing it all the same.

Nobody paid any attention to Halla. She leant against the wall and talked to the Scythian horses who had come with her in the boat. One of them was terribly upset; he had eaten something which had made him ill: the charioteers were always giving queer concoctions to the racehorses which they thought would make them go faster, birds' blood and feathers, for instance, and hot spices. Now this horse, who had been named in Greek, Day-Star, wanted to be quiet and eat nothing for a while and then, when he was better, to eat good grass torn by his own teeth in the field where it grew. But instead his charioteer had forced him to eat something loathsome to horses, the grooms had held his nostrils and shoved the thing down his gasping throat—he

Flora Temple and Princess in Their Great Race, Long Island, 1859, Currier and Ives

[41]

Charioteer and Four Horses, on Greek amphora, 5th century B.C.

shivered all over remembering it. And then they had burnt him here and there with a red-hot iron. They had done this to drive out evil spirits which they thought had made the horse ill and had probably been put into him by a rival. One of the grooms shouted to Halla to stand back; this horse would kick her. But Day-Star was nuzzling against her, and she stroked under his chin and round his ears, saying she would try to tell the grooms. One of them came up with a bucket, and Day-Star, thinking this was some other filthy thing they wanted to force down him, kicked the groom and broke his arm.

The rest came running up and the charioteer with them. The little charioteer was yelling that he was not going to race with a vicious brute like that, and the rest saying he still had the devils in him and running to heat the irons and crack the big hide whips. And Day-Star himself yelled his hate of them all, neighing and striking with his hooves, and the men shouted to Halla to get back quick. But Halla called to them that she would quiet Day-Star if they would let her do what she wanted. So when Day-Star stopped struggling she untied his halter and led him out and gave him a drink of fresh water and praised and petted him. The others stood round at a distance. She told them that if they would not hurt him any more nor make him eat filth, Day-Star would be good.

The charioteer came over very cautiously. He looked at Halla and he looked at Day-Star. Halla said: "Look close. There are no devils in him."

"How did you do it?" whispered the charioteer. "Are you a witch? How much do you want for it?"

"I want that you should be good to Day-Star when he is good. Show him that you mean him no harm."

After a moment the charioteer came up and held out his bare hands to Day-Star who blew at them and smelt them. The charioteer lifted his hand slowly and began to stroke Day-Star's cheeks and neck. They looked at one another in the eyes. The charioteer took a ripe pear out of the fold of his tunic and held it out. Day-Star reached his head forward a little and nibbled at it. Then the charioteer ate a bit, then Day-Star finished it. "He is the best horse I have driven," said the charioteer, "but I was never sure of him."

"Why did you pull him back at the races last week?" asked Halla.

The charioteer looked round. "You know too much," he said. "You are certainly a witch!" Halla said nothing, she was not even quite sure what he meant. "No," he said suddenly. "You are not a witch! I am sorry I said it. But there are things it is best not to say, even if the saints tell one. I will not have to pull Day-Star tomorrow. But will he do the best that is in him?"

"He will do his best if you promise not to give him wrong foods nor to hurt him with whips and irons."

"It was all for his good," said the charioteer, and then, his voice shaken a bit, "I meant it, at least, all for his good."

"He did not think so," said Halla. "Do you promise?"

"Yes, lady," said the charioteer, and put his hand on his heart and bowed, for now he thought that Halla had come at least from his patron saint, and he supposed his mother had been burning candles in his name to the saint, as she sometimes did before a race, and he made up his mind that he would never laugh at her again for doing this. Secretly he said over all the prayers he could remember, and while he did this Halla spoke to Day-Star about the race. Now Day-Star really loved racing and he liked the smell and voice of the little charioteer, but he said that there was a certain groom whose smell he hated, and if he was to do his best, that groom was not to come near him. All the horses hated this man. He told her which one it was and Halla told the charioteer. As this charioteer was a freedman and well paid, and the groom was a slave and not valuable at all, it was easy to have him beaten where Day-Star could see it and then taken out to be sold. Day-Star trembled and whinnied with hate and pleasure, seeing his enemy punished, and so did the other horses, but Halla did not like it somehow.

She asked which horses would be racing against Day-Star and the charioteer told her. He wanted now to tell her everything. He was light-boned and no taller than Halla and he bowed his head over his clasped hands while he spoke to her. She went and talked to all the other horses and got them to agree that Day-Star should win and that they should tell this to the horses from any other of the stables who might be in the same race. Some of them were difficult about it, for they too loved racing; they loved to prance and show off, bouncing the light gilt chariots with the blue or green tunicked charioteers, and their own bodies brushed and combed and glowing so that every hair felt in place and every muscle ready to burst into action. Halla persuaded them that it would work out well for everyone if Day-Star were to win this race; the next race it could be another. The horses said that this might be, but the charioteers drove the chariots across one another and lashed at one another's eyes, and accidents could happen. Yet they could see that it might be best if they had decided among themselves who was to win. And for this time it should be Day-Star.

Halla was afraid they might have forgotten the next morning, but still it was worth trying. So she told Roddin to bet on Day-Star and to bet most of the money they had, and would he buy her a seat for herself close to the starting point. Now they were anxious about this and uncertain whether to take her advice, for how would she know? But at last they put heavy bets on Day-Star

[43]

and bought her the seat. But for themselves, they said they would wait outside, for, if this were to work out, they would not need even to see it, and if it did not work out they would not want to have spent any of the little money they now had left on even the cheapest seats.

Halla got to her place early. In the middle of the audience there was a block of seats raised above the rest, with gilt railings and a silk awning, and in the very best place a wide and soft seat scattered with cushions of gold-embroidered leather, filled with down, and after a time the Emperor came and sat there leaning back. By now Halla had come to understand that the Purple-born was no dragon, but only a little man with thin hands and deep-set dark eyes that never seemed to look at anything and clothes that seemed too heavy and stiff for anybody to bear. He had his guards standing round him, big, tall, fair-haired men with swords and axes, long-jawed and blued-eyed: too like heroes, thought Halla.

Before the chariot races there were entertainments, but many of them were cruel, showing only that some men had power over other men and over beasts. And the other men and the beasts all cried out in various kinds of fear and agony and Halla did not like it, though others, including the Purple-born, seemed to. Then there were smaller races. And at last Day-Star and the other horses, prancing and rearing, and everyone in the Hippodrome shouting and yelling for the horses and the colours they liked. Day-Star's charioteer was a green. With all that noise going on, it was easy enough for Halla to call to the horses, reminding them of what had been said, that Day-Star was to win. And the horses whinnied back, yes, yes, and she hoped they would not get too excited to remember.

In one lap of the race a tough, long-legged mare from one of the blue stables, was ahead of Day-Star for a short time. Then suddenly she dropped back—had she remembered? Day-Star was first round the winning post and Halla saw the charioteer jump down and put an arm up to pull the forelock out of Day-Star's eyes and pet him. She had also noticed that, although he had swung his whip impressively, screaming and shouting as he did so, the lash of it had never fallen on Day-Star. As they came back in triumph to the starting post he neighed at her: I did it, I did it! And the rest of the horses, almost as pleased with themselves as Day-Star, neighed too: We did it, we did it!

FROM

Black Beauty

Anna Sewell

"Now Mr Manly," he said, after carefully looking at us both, "I can see no fault in these horses, but we all know that horses have their peculiarities as well as men, and that sometimes they need different treatment; I should like to know if there is anything particular in either of these, that

The Prince of Wales's Phaeton, George Stubbs

you would like to mention."

"Well," said John, "I don't believe there is a better pair of horses in the country, and right grieved I am to part with them, but they are not alike; the black one is the most perfect temper I ever knew; I suppose he has never known a hard word or a blow since he was foaled, and all his pleasure seems to be to do what you wish; but the chestnut I fancy must have had bad treatment; we heard as much from the dealer. She came to us snappish and suspicious, but when she found what sort of place ours was, it all went off by degrees; for three years I have never seen the smallest sign of temper, and if she is well treated there is not a better, more willing animal than she is; but she is naturally a more irritable constitution than the black horse; flies tease her more; anything wrong in the harness frets her more; and if she were illused or unfairly treated she would not be unlikely to give tit for tat; you know that many high mettled horses will do so."

"Of course," said York, "I quite understand, but you know it is not easy in stables like these to have all the grooms just what they should be; I do my best, and there I must leave it. I'll remember what you have said about the mare."

They were going out of the stable, when John stopped and said, "I had better mention that we have never used the 'bearing rein' with either of them; the black horse never had one on, and the dealer said it was the gag-bit that spoiled the other's temper."

"Well," said York, "if they come here, they must wear the bearing rein. I prefer a loose rein myself, and his lordship is always very reasonable about horses; but my lady—that's another thing, she will have style; and if her carriage horses are not reined up tight, she wouldn't look at them. I always stand out against the gag-bit, and shall do so, but it must be tight up when my lady rides!"

"I am sorry for it, very sorry," said John, "but I must go now, or I shall lose the train."

He came round to each of us to pat and speak to us for the last time; his voice sounded very sad.

I held my face close to him, that was all I could do to say good bye; and then he was gone, and I have never seen him since.

The next day Lord W—— came to look at us; he seemed pleased with our appearance.

"I have great confidence in these horses," he said, "from the character my friend Mr Gordon has given me of them. Of course they are not a match in colour, but my idea is, that they will do very well for the carriage whilst we are in the country. Before we go to London I must try to match Baron; the black horse, I believe, is perfect for riding."

York then told him what John had said about us. "Well," said he, "you must keep an eye to the mare, and put the bearing rein easy; I dare say they will do very well with a little humouring at first. I'll mention it to your lady."

In the afternoon we were harnessed and put in the carriage, and as the stable clock struck three we were led round to the front of the house. It was all very grand, and three or four times as large as the old house at Birtwick, but not half so pleasant, if a horse may have an opinion. Two footmen were standing ready, dressed in drab livery, with scarlet breeches and white stockings. Presently we heard the rustling sound of silk as my lady came down the flight of stone steps. She stepped round to look at us; she was a tall, proud-looking woman, and did not seem pleased about something, but she said nothing, and got into the carriage. This was the first time of wearing a bearing rein, and I must say—though it certainly was a nuisance not to be able to get my head down now and then, it did not pull my head higher than I was accustomed to carry it. I felt anxious about Ginger, but she seemed to be quiet and content.

The next day at three o'clock we were again at the door, and the footmen as before; we heard the silk dress rustle, and the lady came down the steps and in an imperious voice, she said, "York, you must put those horses' heads higher, they are not fit to be seen." York got down and said very respectfully, "I beg you pardon, my lady, but these horses have not been reined up for three years, and my lord said it would be safer to bring them to it by degrees; but if your ladyship pleases, I can take them up a little more."

"Do so," she said.

York came round to our heads and shortened the rein himself, one hole I think; every little makes a difference, be it for better or worse, and that day we had a steep hill to go up. Then I began to understand what I had heard of. Of course I wanted to put my head forward and take the carriage up with a will, as we had been used to do; but no, I had to pull with my head up now, and that took all the spirit out of me, and the strain came on my back and legs. When we came in, Ginger said, "Now you see what it is like, but this is not bad, and if it does not get much worse than this, I shall say nothing about it, for we are very well treated here; but if they strain me up tight, why, let 'em look out! I can't bear it, and I won't."

Day by day, hole by hole our bearing reins were shortened, and instead of looking forward with pleasure to having my harness put on as I used to do, I began to dread it. Ginger too seemed restless, though she said very little. At last I thought the worst was over; for several days there was no more shortening, and I determined to make the best of it and do my duty, though it was now a constant harass instead of a pleasure; but the worst was not come.

One day my lady came down later than usual, and the silk rustled more than ever.

"Drive to the Duchess of B's," she said, and then after a pause—"Are you never going to get those horses' heads up, York? Raise them up at once, and let us have no more of this humouring and nonsense."

York came to me first, whilst the groom stood at Ginger's head. He drew my head back and fixed the rein so tight that it was almost intolerable; then he went to Ginger, who was impatiently

A Gentleman Driving in the Grounds of His Country Estate, F. C. Turner

jerking her head up and down against the bit, as was her way now. She had a good idea of what was coming, and the moment York took the rein off the terret in order to shorten it, she took her opportunity, and reared up so suddenly, that York had his nose roughly hit, and his hat knocked off; the groom was nearly thrown off his legs. At once they both flew to her head, but she was a match for them, and went on plunging, rearing, and kicking in a most desperate manner; at last she kicked right over the carriage pole and fell down, after giving me a severe blow on my near quarter. There is no knowing what further mischief she might have done, had not York promptly sat himself down flat on her head, to prevent her struggling, at the same time calling out, "Unbuckle the black horse! run for the winch and unscrew the carriage pole; cut the trace here— somebody, if you can't unhitch it." One of the footmen ran for the winch, and another brought a knife from the house. The groom soon set me free from Ginger and the carriage, and led me to my box. He just turned me in as I was, and ran back to York. I was much excited by what had happened, and if I had ever been used to kick or rear, I am sure I should have done it then; but I never had, and there I stood angry, sore in my leg, my head still strained up to the terret on the saddle, and no power to get it down. I was very miserable, and felt much inclined to kick the first person who came near me.

Before long, however, Ginger was led in by two grooms, a good deal knocked about and bruised. York came with her and gave his orders, and then came to look at me. In a moment he let down my head.

"Confound these bearing reins!" he said to himself; "I thought we should have some mischief soon—master will be sorely vexed; but there—if a woman's husband can't rule her, of course a servant can't; so I wash my hands of it, and if she can't get to the Duchess' garden party, I can't help it." York did not say this before the men, he always spoke respectfully when they were by. Now, he felt me over, and soon found the place above my hock where I had been kicked. It was swelled and painful; he ordered it to be sponged with hot water, and then some lotion was put on.

Lord W—— was much put out when he learned what had happened; he blamed York for giving way to his mistress, to which he replied, that in future he would much prefer to receive his orders only from his lordship; but I think nothing came of it, for things went on the same as before. I thought York might have stood up better for his horses, but perhaps I am no judge.

Ginger was never put into the carriage again, but when she was well of her bruises, one of Lord W's younger sons said he should like to have her; he was sure she would make a good hunter. As for me, I was obliged still to go in the carriage, and had a fresh partner called Max; he had always been used to the tight rein. I asked him how it was he bore it. "Well," he said, "I bear it because I must, but it is shortening my life, and so it will yours, if you have to stick to it."

"Do you think," I said, "that our masters know how bad it is for us?"

"I can't say," he replied, "but the dealers and the horse doctors know it very well. I was at a dealer's once, who was training me and another horse to go as a pair; he was getting our heads up as he said, a little higher and a little higher everyday. A gentleman who was there asked him why he did so; 'Because,' said he, 'people won't buy them unless we do. The London people always want their horses to carry their heads high, and to step high; of course it is very bad for the horses, but then it is good for trade. The horses soon wear up, or get diseased, and they come for another pair.' That," said Max, "is what he said in my hearing, and you can judge for yourself."

What I suffered with that rein for four long months in my lady's carriage, it would be hard to describe, but I am quite sure that, had it lasted much longer, either my health or my temper would have given way. Before that, I never knew what it was to foam at the mouth, but now the action of the sharp bit on my tongue and jaw, and the constrained position of my head and throat, always caused me to froth at the mouth more or less. Some people think it very fine to see this, and say, "What fine-spirited creatures!" But it is just as unnatural for horses as for men, to foam at the mouth. It is a sure sign of something wrong, and generally proceeds from suffering. Besides this, there was a pressure on my windpipe, which often made my breathing very uncomfortable; when I returned from work, my neck and chest were strained and painful, my mouth and tongue tender, and I felt worn and depressed.

FROM

The Horse and His Boy

C. S. Lewis

"Leave out all these idle words in your own praise," said the Tarkaan. " It is enough to know that you took the child—and have had ten times the worth of his daily bread out of him in labour, as anyone can see. And now tell me at once what price you put on him, for I am wearied with your loquacity."

"You yourself have wisely said," answered Arsheesh, "that the boy's labour has been to me of inestimable value. This must be taken into account in fixing the price. For if I sell the boy I must undoubtedly either buy or hire another to do his work."

"I'll give you fifteen crescents for him," said the Tarkaan.

"Fifteen!" cried Arsheesh in a voice that was something between a whine and a scream. "Fifteen! For the prop of my old age and the delight of my eyes! Do not mock my grey beard, Tarkaan though you be. My price is seventy."

At this point Shasta got up and tiptoed away. He had heard all he wanted, for he had often listened when men were bargaining in the village and knew how it was done. He was quite certain that Arsheesh would sell him in the end for something much more than fifteen crescents and much less than seventy, but that he and the Tarkaan would take hours in getting to an agreement.

You must not imagine that Shasta felt at all as you and I would feel if we had just overheard our parents talking about selling us for slaves. For one thing, his life was already little better than slavery; for all he knew, the lordly stranger on the great horse might be kinder to him than Arsheesh. For another, the story about his own discovery in the boat had filled him with excitement and with a sense of relief. He had often been uneasy because, try as he might, he had never been able to love the fisherman, and he knew that a boy ought to love his father. And now, apparently, he was no relation to Arsheesh at all. That took a great weight off his mind. "Why,

Raja Ranjit Singh of Jaisalman

I might be anyone!" he thought. "I might be the son of a Tarkaan myself—or the son of the Tisroc (may he live forever)—or of a god!"

He was standing out in the grassy place before the cottage while he thought these things. Twilight was coming on apace and a star or two was already out, but the remains of the sunset could still be seen in the west. Not far away the stranger's horse, loosely tied to an iron ring in the wall of the donkey's stable, was grazing. Shasta strolled over to it and patted its neck. It went on tearing up the grass and took no notice of him.

Then another thought came into Shasta's mind. "I wonder what sort of a man that Tarkaan is," he said out loud. "It would be splendid if he was kind. Some of the slaves in a great lord's house have next to nothing to do. They wear lovely clothes and eat meat every day. Perhaps he'd take me to the wars and I'd save his life in a battle and then he'd set me free and adopt me as his son and give me a palace and a chariot and a suit of armour. But then he might be a horrid, cruel man. He might send me to work on the fields in chains. I wish I knew. How can I know? I bet this horse knows, if only he could tell me."

The Horse had lifted its head. Shasta stroked its smooth-as-satin nose and said, "I wish *you* could talk, old fellow."

And then for a second he thought he was dreaming, for quite distinctly, though in a low voice, the Horse said, "But I can."

Shasta stared into its great eyes and his own grew almost as big, with astonishment.

"How ever did *you* learn to talk?" he asked.

"Hush! Not so loud," replied the Horse. "Where I come from, nearly all the animals talk."

"Wherever is that?" asked Shasta.

"Narnia," answered the Horse. "The happy land of Narnia—Narnia of the heathery mountains and the thymy downs, Narnia of the many rivers, the plashing glens, the mossy caverns and the deep forests ringing with the hammers of the Dwarfs. Oh the sweet air of Narnia! An hour's life there is better than a thousand years in Calormen." It ended with a whinny that sounded very like a sigh.

"How did you get here?" said Shasta.

"Kidnapped," said the Horse. "Or stolen, or captured—whichever you like to call it. I was only a foal at the time. My mother warned me not to range the southern slopes, into Archenland and beyond, but I wouldn't heed her. And by the Lion's Mane I have paid for my folly. All these years I have been a slave to humans, hiding my true nature and pretending to be dumb and witless like *their* horses."

"Why didn't you tell them who you were?"

"Not such a fool, that's why. If they'd once found out I could talk they would have made a show of me at fairs and guarded me more carefully than ever. My last chance of escape would have been gone."

"And why—" began Shasta, but the Horse interrupted him.

"Now look," it said, "we mustn't waste time on idle questions. You want to know about my master the Tarkaan Anradin. Well, he's bad. Not too bad to me, for a war horse costs too much to be treated very badly. But you'd better be lying dead tonight than to go to be a human slave in his house tomorrow."

"Then I'd better run away," said Shasta, turning very pale.

"Yes, you had," said the Horse. "But why not run away with me?"

"Are you going to run away too?" said Shasta.

"Yes, if you'll come with me," answered the Horse. "This is the chance for both of us. You see if I run away without a rider, everyone who sees me will say 'Stray horse' and be after me as quick as he can. With a rider I've a chance to get through. That's where you can help me. On the other hand, you can't get very far on those two silly legs of yours (what absurd legs humans have!) without being overtaken. But on me you can outdistance any other horse in this country. That's where I can help you. By the way, I suppose you know how to ride?"

"Oh yes, of course," said Shasta. "At least, I've ridden the donkey."

"Ridden the *what*?" retorted the Horse with extreme contempt. (At least, that is what he meant. Actually it came out in a sort of neigh—"Ridden the wha-ha-ha-ha." Talking horses always become more horsy in accent when they are angry.)

"In other words," it continued, "you *can't* ride. That's a drawback. I'll have to teach you as we go along. If you can't ride, can you fall?"

"I suppose anyone can fall," said Shasta.

"I mean can you fall and get up again without crying and mount again and fall again and yet not be afraid of falling?"

"I—I'll try," said Shasta.

"Poor little beast," said the Horse in a gentler tone. "I forget you're only a foal. We'll make a fine rider of you in time. And now—we mustn't start until those two in the hut are asleep. Meantime we can make our plans. My Tarkaan is on his way North to the great city, to Tashbaan itself and the court of the Tisroc—"

"I say," put in Shasta in rather a shocked voice, "oughtn't you to say 'May he live for ever?'"

"Why?" asked the Horse. "I'm a free Narnian. And why should I talk slaves' and fools' talk? I don't want him to live for ever, and I know that he's not going to live for ever whether I want him to or not. And I can see you're from the free North too. No more of this Southern jargon between you and me! And now, back to our plans. As I said, my human was on his way North to Tashbaan."

"Does that mean we'd better go to the South?"

"I think not," said the Horse. "You see, he thinks I'm dumb and witless like his other horses. Now if I really were, the moment I got loose I'd go back home to my stable and paddock; back to his palace which is two days' journey South. That's where he'll look for me. He'd never dream of my going on North on my own. And anyway he will probably think that someone in the last village who saw him ride through has followed us to here and stolen me."

"Oh hurrah!" said Shasta. "Then we'll go North. I've been longing to go to the North all my life."

"Of course you have," said the Horse. "That's because of the blood that's in you. I'm sure you're true Northern stock. But not too loud. I should think they'd be asleep soon now."

"I'd better creep back and see," suggested Shasta.

"That's a good idea," said the Horse. "But take care you're not caught."

It was a good deal darker now and very silent except for the sound of the waves on the beach, which Shasta hardly noticed because he had been hearing it day and night as long as he could remember. The cottage, as he approached it, showed no light. When he listened at the front there was no noise. When he went round to the only window, he could hear, after a second or two, the familiar noise of the old fisherman's squeaky snore. It was funny to think that if all went well he would never hear it again. Holding his breath and feeling a little bit sorry, but much less sorry than he was glad, Shasta glided away over the grass and went to the donkey's stable, groped along to a place he knew where the key was hidden, opened the door and found the Horse's saddle and bridle which had been locked up there for the night. He bent forward and kissed the donkey's nose. "I'm sorry we can't take *you*," he said.

"There you are at last," said the Horse when he got back to it. "I was beginning to wonder what had become of you."

"I was getting your things out of the stable," replied Shasta. "And now, can you tell me how to put them on?"

For the next few minutes Shasta was at work, very cautiously to avoid jingling, while the Horse said things like, "Get that girth a bit tighter," or "You'll find a buckle lower down," or "You'll need to shorten those stirrups a good bit." When all was finished it said:

"Now; we've got to have reins for the look of the thing, but you won't be using them. Tie them to the saddle-bow: very slack so that I can do what I like with my head. And, remember—you are not to touch them."

"What are they for, then?" asked Shasta.

"Ordinarily they are for directing me," replied the Horse. "But as I intend to do all the directing on this journey, you'll please keep your hands to yourself. And there's another thing. I'm not going to have you grabbing my mane."

"But I say," pleaded Shasta. "If I'm not to hold on by the reins or by your mane, what *am* I to hold on by?"

"You hold on with your knees," said the Horse. "That's the secret of good riding. Grip my body between your knees as hard as you like; sit straight up, straight as a poker; keep your elbows in. And by the way, what did you do with the spurs?"

"Put them on my heels, of course," said Shasta. "I do know that much."

"Then you can take them off and put them in the saddlebag. We may be able to sell them when we get to Tashbaan. Ready? And now I think you can get up."

"Ooh! You're a dreadful height," gasped Shasta after his first, and unsuccessful, attempt.

"I'm a horse, that's all," was the reply. "Anyone would think I was a haystack from the way you're trying to climb up me! There, that's better. Now sit *up* and remember what I told you about your knees. Funny to think of me who has led cavalry charges and won races having a potato-sack like you in the saddle! However, off we go." It chuckled, not unkindly.

And it certainly began their night journey with great caution. First of all it went just south of the fisherman's cottage to the little river which there ran into the sea, and took care to leave in the mud some very plain hoof-marks pointing South. But as soon as they were in the middle of the ford it turned upstream and waded till they were about a hundred yards farther inland than the cottage. Then it selected a nice gravelly bit of bank which would take no footprints and came out

Man on a Horse, Henri Gaudier-Brzeska

[53]

on the Northern side. Then, still at a walking pace, it went Northward till the cottage, the one tree, the donkey's stable, and the creek—everything, in fact, that Shasta had ever known—had sunk out of sight in the grey summer-night darkness. They had been going uphill and now were at the top of the ridge—that ridge which had always been the boundary of Shasta's known world. He could not see what was ahead except that it was all open and grassy. It looked endless: wild and lonely and free.

"I say!" observed the Horse. "What a place for a gallop, eh?"

"Oh don't let's," said Shasta. "Not yet. I don't know how to—please, Horse. I don't know your name."

"Breehy-hinny-brinny-hoohy-hah," said the Horse.

"I'll never be able to say that," said Shasta. "Can I call you Bree?"

"Well, if it's the best you can do, I suppose you must," said the Horse. "And what shall I call you?"

"I'm called Shasta."

"H'm," said Bree. "Well, now, there's a name that's *really* hard to pronounce. But now about this gallop. It's a good deal easier than trotting if you only knew, because you don't have to rise and fall. Grip with your knees and keep your eyes straight ahead between my ears. Don't look at the ground. If you think you're going to fall just grip harder and sit up straighter. Ready? Now: for Narnia and the North."

FROM

Gulliver's Travels

Jonathan Swift

In the midst of this distress I observed [these human-looking creatures] all to run away on a sudden as fast as they could, at which I ventured to leave the tree, and pursue the road, wondering what it was that could put them into this fright. But looking on my left hand I saw a horse walking softly in the fields; which my persecutors having sooner discovered, was the cause of their flight. The horse started a little when he came near me, but soon recovering himself looked full in my face with manifest tokens of wonder; he viewed my hands and feet, walking round me several times. I would have pursued my journey, but he placed himself directly in the way, yet looking with a very mild aspect, never offering the least violence. We stood gazing at each other for some time; at last I took the boldness to reach my hand towards his neck, with a design to stroke it, using the common style and whistle of jockeys when they are going to handle a strange horse. But

Phantasy, Henry Lamb

this animal seeming to receive my civilities with disdain, shook his head, and bent his brows, softly raising up his right fore-foot to remove my hand. Then he neighed three or four times, but in so different a cadence, that I almost began to think he was speaking to himself in some language of his own.

While he and I were thus employed, another horse came up; who applying himself to the first in a very formal manner, they gently struck each other's right hoof before, neighing several times by turns, and varying the sound, which seemed to be almost articulate. They went some paces off, as if it were to confer together, walking side by side, backward and forward, like persons deliberating upon some affair of weight but often turning their eyes towards me, as it were to watch that I might not escape. I was amazed to see such actions and behaviour in brute beasts, and concluded with myself, that if the inhabitants of this country were endued with a proportionable degree of reason, they must needs be the wisest people upon earth. This thought gave me so much comfort, that I resolved to go forward until I could discover some house or

Mazeppa Surrounded by Horses, John Frederick Herring Senior

village, or meet with any of the natives, leaving the two horses to discourse together as they pleased. But the first, who was a dapple grey, observing me to steal off, neighed after me in so expressive a tone, that I fancied myself to understand what he meant, whereupon I turned back, and came near him, to expect his farther commands, but concealing my fear as much as I could, for I began to be in some pain, how this adventure might terminate; and the reader will easily believe I did not much like my present situation.

The two horses came up close to me, looking with great earnestness upon my face and hands. The grey steed rubbed my hat all round with his right fore-hoof, and discomposed it so much that I was forced to adjust it better by taking it off, and settling it again; whereat both he and his companion (who was a brown bay) appeared to be much surprised; the latter felt the lappet of my coat, and finding it to hang loose about me, they both looked with new signs of wonder. He stroked my right hand, seeming to admire the softness and colour, but he squeezed it so hard between his hoof and his pastern, that I was forced to roar; after which they both touched me with all possible tenderness. They were under great perplexity about my shoes and stockings, which they felt very often, neighing to each other, and using various gestures, not unlike those of a philosopher, when he would attempt to solve some new and difficult phenomenon.

Upon the whole, the behaviour of these animals was so orderly and rational, so acute and judicious, that I at last concluded they must needs be magicians, who had thus metamorphosed themselves upon some design, and seeing a stranger in the way, were resolved to divert themselves with him; or perhaps were really amazed at the sight of a man so very different in habit, feature and complexion from those who might probably live in so remote a climate. Upon the strength of this reasoning, I ventured to address them in the following manner: Gentlemen, if you be conjurers, as I have good cause to believe, you can understand any language; therefore I make bold to let your worships know that I am a poor distressed Englishman, driven by his misfortunes upon your coast, and I entreat one of you, to let me ride upon his back, as if he were a real horse, to some house or village where I can be relieved. In return of which favour I will make you a present of this knife and bracelet (taking them out of my pocket). The two creatures stood silent while I spoke, seeming to listen with great attention; and when I had ended, they neighed frequently towards each other, as if they were engaged in serious conversation. I plainly observed, that their language expressed the passions very well, and the words might with little pains be resolved into an alphabet more easily than the Chinese.

I could frequently distinguish the word *Yahoo*, which was repeated by each of them several times; and although it was impossible for me to conjecture what it meant, yet while the two horses were busy in conversation, I endeavoured to practise this word upon my tongue; and as soon as they were silent, I boldly pronounced *Yahoo* in a loud voice, imitating, at the same time, as near as I could, the neighing of a horse, at which they were both visibly surprised, and the grey repeated the same word twice, as if he meant to teach me the right accent, wherein I spoke after him as well as I could, and found myself perceivably to improve every time, though very far from any degree of perfection. Then the bay tried me with a second word, much harder to be pronounced; but reducing it to the English orthography, may be spelt thus, *Houyhnhnm*. I did not succeed in this so well as the former, but after two or three further trials, I had better fortune and they both appeared amazed at my capacity.

After some further discourse, which I then conjectured might relate to me, the two friends took their leaves, with the same compliment of striking each other's hoof; and the grey made me signs that I should walk before him whereon I thought it prudent to comply, till I could find a better director. When I offered to slacken my pace, he would cry *Hhuun Hhuun*; I guessed his meaning and gave him to understand as well as I could, that I was weary, and not able to walk

ودزدواره برايد ونوتى نال كشى كند وماده جهل اكن خورد وناست نال كى بايد وعمر كند
هل اوج نال كشد فرجو زبر ماذيار آبستر جهر كزماه كره ماه كرده اند والراست بهد زيار بدارد از هرآنك

اب فرد رست دندان هه جانو دار دزيرى نسياه شود الاد يدان اسب كه سبيد و دوش كردد
وارسا فع او دماغ اسب زا باصير وبود زوعست ابراآسر جو سابد تابا هم آدم مرهى جنو ب
باشد جهت نامت جراحات زا بكر او زآخ او ند بر قان بوى كه دسحت مقد مانند ذهن او زابامير نز

Mare, from the Manafi' al-Hayawan

faster; upon which he would stand a while to let me rest.

Having travelled about three miles, we came to a long kind of building, made of timber stuck in the ground, and wattled across; the roof was low, and covered with straw. I now began to be a little comforted, and took out some toys, which travellers usually carry for presents to the savage Indians of America and other parts, in hopes the people of the house would be thereby encouraged to receive me kindly. The horse made me a sign to go in first; it was a large room with a smooth clay floor, and a rack and manger extending the whole length on one side. There were three nags, and two mares, not eating, but some of them sitting down upon their hams, which I very much wondered at; but wondered more to see the rest employed in domestic business. These seemed but ordinary cattle; however, this confirmed my first opinion, that a people who could so far civilize brute animals, must needs excel in wisdom all the nations of the world. The grey came in just after, and thereby prevented any ill treatment which the others might have given me. He neighed to them several times in a style of authority, and received answers.

Beyond this room there were three others, reaching the length of the house, to which you passed through three doors, opposite to each other, in the manner of a vista; we went through the second room towards the third; here the grey walked in first, beckoning me to attend. I waited in the second room, and got ready my presents for the master and mistress of the house; they were two knives, three bracelets of false pearl, a small looking-glass, and a bead necklace. The horse neighed three or four times, and I waited to hear some answers in a human voice, but I heard no other returns than in the same dialect, only one or two a little shriller than his. I began to think that this house must belong to some person of great note among them, because there appeared so much ceremony before I could gain admittance. But, that a man of quality should be served all by horses, was beyond my comprehension. I feared my brain was disturbed by my sufferings and misfortunes: I roused myself, and looked about me in the room where I was left alone; this was furnished like the first, only after a more elegant manner. I rubbed my eyes often, but the same objects still occurred. I pinched my arms and sides to awake myself, hoping I might be in a dream. I then absolutely concluded, that all these appearances could be nothing else but necromancy and magic. But I had no time to pursue these reflections; for the grey horse came to the door, and made me a sign to follow him into the third room, where I saw a very comely mare, together with a colt and foal, sitting on their haunches, upon mats of straw, not unartfully made, and perfectly neat and clean.

The mare soon after my entrance, rose from her mat, and coming up close, after having nicely observed my hands and face, gave me a most contemptuous look; then turning to the horse, I heard the word *Yahoo* often repeated betwixt them; the meaning of which word I could not then comprehend, although it were the first I had learned to pronounce; but I was soon better informed, to my everlasting mortification: for the horse beckoning to me with his head, and repeating the word *Hhuun, Hhuun,* as he did upon the road, which I understood was to attend him, led me out into a kind of court, where was another building at some distance from the house. Here we entered, and I saw three of these detestable creatures, whom I first met after my landing, feeding upon roots, and the flesh of some animals, which I afterwards found to be that of asses and dogs, and now and then a cow dead by accident or disease. They were all tied by the neck with strong withes, fastened to a beam; they held their food between the claws of their fore-feet, and tore it with their teeth.

The master horse ordered a sorrel nag, one of his servants, to untie the largest of these animals, and take him into the yard. The beast and I were brought close together, and our countenances diligently compared, both by master and servant, who thereupon repeated several times the word *Yahoo.* My horror and astonishment are not to be described, when I observed in this abominable animal a perfect human figure: the face of it indeed was flat and broad, the nose depressed, the lips large, and the mouth wide. But these differences are common to all savage nations, where the lineaments of the countenance are distorted by the natives suffering their infants to lie grovelling on the earth, or by carrying them on their backs, nuzzling with their face against the mother's shoulders. The fore-feet of the Yahoo differed from my hands in nothing else but the length of the nails, the coarseness and brownness of the palms, and the hairiness on the backs. There was the same resemblance between our feet, with the same differences, which I knew very well, though the horses did not, because of my shoes and stockings, the same in every part of our bodies, except as to hairiness and colour, which I have already described.

4

All the Sporting Breeds

There is no secret so close as that between a rider and his horse.

from Mr Sponge's Sporting Tour *by R. S. Surtees*

All the Breeds

Dorothy Wellesley

Who, in the garden-pony carry skeps
Of grass or fallen leaves, his knees gone slack,
Round belly, hollow back,
Sees the Mongolian Tarpan of the Steppes?
Or, the Shire with plaits and feathered feet,
The war-horse like the wind the Tartar knew?
Or, in the Suffolk Punch, spells out anew
The wild grey asses fleet
With stripe from head to tail, and moderate ears?
In cross sea-donkeys, sheltering as storm gathers,
The mountain zebras maned upon the withers,
With round enormous ears?

And who in thoroughbreds in stable garb
Of blazoned rug, ranged orderly, will mark
The wistful eyelashes so long and dark
And call to mind the old blood of the Barb?
And that slim island on whose bare campaigns
Galloped with flying manes
For a king's pleasure, churning surf and scud,
A white Arabian stud?

That stallion, teazer to Hobgoblin, free
And foaled upon a plain of Barbary:
Godolphin Barb, who dragged a cart for hire
In Paris, but became a famous sire,
Covering all lovely mares, and she who threw
Rataplan to the Baron, loveliest-shrew;
King Charles's royal mares; the Dodsworth Dam;
And the descendants: Yellow Turk, King Tom;
And Lath out of Roxana, famous foal;
Careless; Eclipse, unbeaten in the race,
With white blaze on his face;
Prunella who was dam to Parasol.

[63]

A Horse Frightened by Lightning, Théodore Géricault

Blood Arab, pony, pedigree, no name,
All horses are the same:
The Shetland stallion stunted by the damp,
Yet filled with self-importance, stout and small;
The Cleveland slow and tall;
New Forests that may ramp
Their lives out, being branded, breeding free
When bluebells turn the Forest to a sea,
When mares with foal at foot flee down the glades,
Sheltering in bramble coverts
From mobs of corn-fed lovers;
Or, at the acorn harvest, in stockades
A round-up being afoot, will stand at bay,
Or, making for the heather clearings, splay

Wide-spread towards the bogs by gorse and whin,
Roped as they flounder in
By foresters.

But hunters as day fails
Will take the short-cut home across the fields;
With slackening rein will stoop through darkening wealds;
With creaking leathers skirt the swedes and kales;
Patient, adventurous still,
A horse's ears bob on the distant hill;
He starts to hear
A pheasant chuck or whirr, having the fear
In him of ages filled with war and raid,
Night gallop, ambuscade;
Remembering adventures of his kin
With giant winged worms that coiled round mountain bases,
And Nordic tales of young gods riding races
Up courses of the rainbow; here, within
The depth of Hampshire hedges, does he dream
How Athens woke, to hear above her roofs
The welkin flash and thunder to the hoofs
Of Dawn's tremendous team?

FROM

A Letter to James Crawford

Horace Walpole

Paris, March 6, 1766

Your Ministers may not know it, but the war has been on the point of breaking out here between France and England, and upon a cause very English—a horse race. Lord Forbes and Lauragais were the champions; they rode, but the second lost. His horse being ill, it died that night, and the surgeons on opening it swore it was poisoned. The English suspect that a groom, who I suppose

The Match Between Aaron and Driver, 1754, Richard Roper

had been reading Livy or Demosthenes, poisoned it on patriotic principles, to insure victory to his country. The French, on the contrary, think poison as common as oats or beans in the stables at Newmarket. In short, there is no impertinence they have not uttered, and it has gone so far that two nights ago it was said that the King had forbidden another race, which is appointed for Monday, between the Prince de Nassau and a Mr Forth, to prevent national animosities. On my side I have tried to stifle these heats, by threatening them that Mr Pitt is coming into the Ministry again; and it has had some effect. This event has confirmed what I discovered early after my arrival, that the *Anglomanie* was worn out; if it remains, it is *manie* against the English.

The Brigadier

John Hislop

For some time we had been considering the possibility of running the Brigadier in the King George VI and the Queen Elizabeth Stakes, and when Mill Reef was announced a non-runner in the Eclipse Stakes we decided that this race would be a stepping-stone towards the more important and greater prize, at Ascot. We kept quiet about the plan, as we wanted to get the Eclipse Stakes safely over before we made any announcement about the Ascot race.

By now the Brigadier had been undefeated in fourteen starts, two less than the unbeaten record established by Ribot, in whose case several victories were achieved in Italy against local opposition of no great quality, whereas every race contested by the Brigadier was the feature of the day.

Though Mill Reef was not to be in the field, the opposition included some of the best middle-distance horses in Europe, whose riders were certain to ensure that the race was run from start to finish, in order to test the Brigadier's stamina to the utmost. This was the crucial point of the venture since the Brigadier would be racing for the first time over a mile and a half, a distance beyond the expectation suggested by his pedigree.

Thus there was a grave chance that the Brigadier might meet his first defeat. But I have always contended that owners in this country place too much emphasis on defeat and not enough on proving horses thoroughly; and that to be beaten honourably carries more merit than preserving an undefeated record by avoiding the issue. Having expounded this theory forcibly and frequently as a journalist, it would have amounted to flouting my own principles if, when faced with the opportunity, I did not put them into practice.

Therefore we decided that the Brigadier would take his chance, win, lose or draw; and we knew that whatever the outcome he would emerge with credit.

In accordance with his usual practice, Dick did not alter his method of training the Brigadier, despite the fact that he was going to race over a longer distance, keeping him to work around seven furlongs. He blossomed in the warm weather, worked with zest and when he left for Ascot I think he was better than he had ever been in his life.

A vital aspect of the race was that of riding tactics. Ascot is a tricky course in that it is essential, in nine cases out of ten, to be on the heels of the leaders turning into the straight. This makes it dangerous to hold a horse up for a late run or come from some way back, though such tactics are usually favourable to horses of doubtful stamina.

We resolved that the best plan would be for Joe to ride the Brigadier on the assumption that he stayed the distance, relying on his class to enable him to be immediately behind the leaders turning into the straight while still on the bit and open up a lead of a couple of lengths or so, hoping that the momentum of his finishing run, together with his courage, would carry him past the post before his opponents could get to him. The fact that the final twenty yards or so are slightly downhill would help him if his stamina was beginning to give out towards the end.

The day, Saturday 22 July, was fine after some overnight rain and the going officially described as good.

The field was one of the best ever to contest the race, since it included no less than five classic winners, from England, France, Ireland and Italy.

The runners in their order on the racecard were Brigadier Gerard (Joe Mercer) drawn No. 1 on the extreme outside, Fair World (Frankie Durr) drawn No. 4, Parnell (Willie Carson)

Brigadier Gerard, John Steading

The First Futurity, Sheepshead Bay, Brooklyn, 1888, L. Maurer

drawn No. 3, Selhurst (Geoff Lewis) drawn No. 5, Bog Road (Jimmy Lindley) drawn No. 6, Gay Lussac (Lester Piggott) drawn No. 8, Riverman (Freddie Head) drawn No. 7, Steel Pulse (Bill Williamson) drawn No. 9 and Sukawa (Yves Saint-Martin) drawn No. 2.

I was particularly interested to see the French colt Riverman and the unbeaten Italian Derby winner Gay Lussac, on neither of whom I had set eyes before. Riverman, the best horse in France up to ten furlongs, was a sturdy, handsome, medium-sized brown colt by Mill Reef's sire, Never Bend, and was turned out with the customary Alec Head polish. A good looker, he had not quite the best of forelegs and knees, nor the scope of the Brigadier. On his pedigree I doubted his staying a mile and a half, though the same might have been said of the Brigadier.

Gay Lussac was a rangy, lanky chestnut, with an honest head, biggish ears and very clean limbs. He was a shade long in the back and had a fair amount of daylight under him, but looked extremely well and a racehorse of class. Despite his being closely inbred to Nasrullah, he bore no resemblance to the latter whatsoever. Lester Piggott, who was on Gay Lussac, had been over to Italy to ride him work and was reported to have been deeply impressed with the gallop he put up. By Fabergé II out of a mare by Red God, Gay Lussac could not be said to have a mile-and-a-half pedigree and probably won at this distance on his class rather than through genuine stamina.

Steel Pulse and Parnell both looked the part. Steel Pulse, despite his worthy success in the Irish Sweeps Derby, had five lengths and an additional four pounds to make up on the Brigadier on their running in the Prince of Wales Stakes. Parnell, a neat, attractive, chestnut—"He's never

[69]

heard of Brigadier Gerard," his lad quipped to me as he passed—had won the Prix Jean Prat and run second to Rock Roi in the Prix du Cadran (the French equivalent of the Ascot Gold Cup); whatever he did, he would not fail through lack of stamina and was turned out by Bernard van Cutsem looking really well. But none, either in looks or condition, surpassed the Brigadier.

Eclipse, George Stubbs

He was never any trouble to saddle, his only peculiarity being that he disliked the sponge being thrust into his mouth when it was washed out; so Buster used to encourage him to play with it and thus persuade him to tolerate the operation.

Though the day was hot, the Brigadier was as cool as ice, his immaculate appearance causing him to harden in the betting from 11 to 8 on to 13 to 8 on. Had the race been ten furlongs or a mile, this would have been a remarkably generous price, but the fact that he had never run beyond ten furlongs and was going to have his stamina tested to the full accounted for the

A Mongol Horseman, of the Ming dynasty

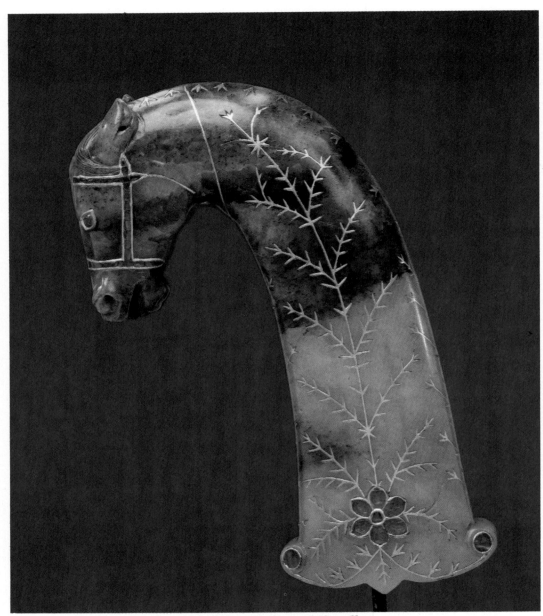

Moghul jade *Sword Handle*

bookmakers' apparent magnanimity. Next in the betting was the Italian colt, Gay Lussac, at fives, then Riverman at 17 to 2, Selhurst at 12 to 1, Steel Pulse at 14 to 1, Parnell and the French outsider, Sukawa, at 28 to 1, and the remaining two, Fair World and Bog Road, 66 to 1.

I was not sorry that the Brigadier had been drawn on the outside, as it would ensure him being free of interference in the first furlong or so and enable Joe to sort out his position as he wanted during the early stages of the race. While it was important that the Brigadier was on the heels of the leaders turning into the straight, it was equally important for Joe not to make too much use of him in the first six furlongs, so that he had as much reserve as possible for the final battle.

The pattern of the race developed exactly as we had hoped, apart from the fast pace throughout, which was not to the Brigadier's advantage but was an eventuality we had accepted as inevitable.

Selhurst was the first to show in front and, in Jim Joel's famous and distinctive "black, scarlet cap", held the lead for the first five furlongs. Bunched behind him were Parnell, Sukawa, Gay Lussac and Steel Pulse. The Brigadier was among the last group, but there was not a great deal spanning the whole field at that stage. He was moving very easily, with a clear run on the outside available to him. In this position Joe had all his chief rivals under his eye and could make an instant appreciation of whatever tactical situation developed.

After five furlongs Willie Carson drove Parnell into the lead, keeping him going vigorously to make the utmost use of his stamina.

From half way the Brigadier began to improve his position until in no time, it seemed, he was in second place behind Parnell as they came into the final bend.

So impressively had the manoeuvre been carried out that from this moment Dick and I, who were standing together on the owners' and trainers' stand, felt that the Brigadier was sure to win. Though Parnell was still galloping strongly and could be relied on to keep going to the end, he did not possess the Brigadier's devastating speed and ability to quicken; and since Joe as yet had been required to do no more than sit still, he would be able to use the Brigadier's most formidable armament with effect.

After turning into the straight, the Brigadier had two lengths to make up and set about it with his wonted determination. It took him a furlong to catch and master Parnell, who showed no sign of stopping but had not the speed to cope with the Brigadier's challenge.

As the Brigadier gained the lead, the cheering of the vast crowd grew in volume and intensity to a roar such as can seldom have been heard over Ascot Heath. Having struck the front he veered towards the rails, probably wishing to race along them as he liked to do. At the same time, Parnell hung towards the centre of the course. Once in command, the Brigadier was never in danger of being caught and passed the post with a length and a half to spare.

Riverman came from a long way back to take third place, five lengths behind Parnell, then Steel Pulse and Gay Lussac. Thus the five classic winners in the race took the first five places. The time, 2m 32.91s, was only .37s slower than that taken in 1971 by Mill Reef, who as a three-year-old carried a stone less.

It was a thoroughly English victory from a truly international field and the Brigadier was given a tremendous ovation as he returned to the winner's enclosure. But hardly had the applause died down than it was announced that there was a stewards' enquiry. Since Parnell and the Brigadier had changed places in the straight, this was understandable; however, as the Brigadier had won on merit and, so far as I could discern and on Joe Mercer's opinion, Parnell had suffered no interference, I was not unduly perturbed at the announcement. But as the minutes went by and no verdict was given out, I began to grow anxious, fearing that the patrol camera might have

The Jockey, Henri de Toulouse-Lautrec

revealed something against the Brigadier which I had not noticed.

To escape the crowd of journalists and others who had gathered outside the weighing room, and in order to endure the suspense in cooler and calmer surroundings, I went into the weighing room and found myself standing next to Seamus McGrath, owner-trainer of Bog Road, winner of the Gallinule Stakes earlier in the season but unsuited to the fast ground at Ascot. We stood chatting about the race and one thing and another, which helped to ease the mounting tension;

eventually an official gave me the glad news that all was well, the placings remaining unaltered.

Though the Brigadier had edged in the direction of the far rails, the patrol camera revealed that Parnell had been left plenty of room to come through, if he had been able to do so; also that Parnell himself had come off a true line, veering towards the centre of the course. A point of interest is that one of the French stewards' secretaries, who was present, expressed the opinion that the Brigadier would still have kept the race had it been in France, where the rule governing interference is much stricter than it is in England.

The Brigadier's victory in the King George VI and the Queen Elizabeth Stakes put the mark of indisputable greatness on him as a racehorse. He had now proved his supremacy from five furlongs to one and a half miles, had beaten the best horses in Europe and, like his famous ancestor Fairway, had won in the topmost class at a distance beyond the expectation of his pedigree.

Standing in the winner's enclosure, a fitting tribute to his merit and courage, he was flawless in his beauty. Bred in England in the face of competition against all the wealth and resources of the foremost studs in America and Europe, he embodied that fusion of the best qualities of a racehorse only to be found in a champion of champions. Though in law he belonged to Jean and to me, in spirit he belonged to England: to all who stood in admiration around him, to the thousands who followed his career and had never seen him, even to those ignorant of his name. In him every Englishman justly could take an equal pride, for he was part of our heritage, evolved from three hundred years of thought and endeavour by those dedicated to perfecting the breed of the racehorse. As I watched him walk away, my heart full of gratitude and joy, I felt— more than pride of achievement—the humility and awe of one chosen by fate to cause this, perhaps the best English racehorse of the century, to be brought into the world and to have in my hand the power to direct his future.

At this moment of his career the Brigadier stood at a pinnacle of achievement unsurpassed by any English racehorse of my time. Indeed only the Italian champion, Ribot, had beaten, by one, his record of fifteen wins in fifteen runs. Apart from lowering Ribot's record and winning the Prix de l'Arc de Triomphe there was little he could do to add to his fame.

FROM

A Farewell to Arms

Ernest Hemingway

One day in the afternoon we went to the races. Ferguson went too and Crowell Rodgers, the boy who had been wounded in the eyes by the explosion of the shell nose-cap. The girls dressed to go after lunch, while Crowell and I sat on the bed in his room and read the past performances of the horses and the predictions in the racing paper. Crowell's head was bandaged and he did not care much about these races but read the racing paper constantly and kept track of all the horses for something to do. He said the horses were a terrible lot but they were all the horses we had. Old Meyers liked him and gave him tips. Meyers won on nearly every race but disliked to give tips because it brought down the prices. The racing was very crooked. Men who had been ruled off the turf everywhere else were racing in Italy. Meyers' information was good but I hated to ask him because sometimes he did not answer, and always you could see it hurt him to tell you, but he felt obligated to tell us for some reason and he hated less to tell Crowell. Crowell's eyes had been hurt, one was hurt badly, and Meyers had trouble with his eyes and so he liked Crowell. Meyers never told his wife what horses he was playing and she won or lost, mostly lost, and talked all the time.

We four drove out to San Siro in an open carriage. It was a lovely day, and we drove out through the park and out along the tramway and out of the town where the road was dusty. There were villas with iron fences and big overgrown gardens and ditches with water flowing and green vegetable gardens with dust on the leaves. We could look across the plain and see farmhouses and the rich green farms with their irrigation ditches and the mountains to the north. There were many carriages going into the race-track, and the men at the gate let us in without cards because we were in uniform. We left the carriage, bought programmes, and walked across the infield and then across the smooth thick turf of the course to the paddock. The grand-stands were old and made of wood and the betting booths were under the stands and in a row out near the stables. There was a crowd of soldiers along the fence in the infield. The paddock was fairly well filled with people and they were walking the horses around in a ring under the trees behind the grand-stand. We saw people we knew and got chairs for Ferguson and Catherine and watched the horses.

They went around one after the other, their heads down, the grooms leading them. One horse, a purplish black, Crowell swore was dyed that color. We watched him and it seemed possible. He had only come out just before the bell rang to saddle. We looked him up in the program from the number on the groom's arm and it was listed a black gelding named Japalac. The race was for horses that had never won a race worth one thousand lire or more. Catherine was sure his color had been changed. Ferguson said she could not tell. I thought he looked suspicious. We all agreed we ought to back him and pooled one hundred lire. The odds sheets showed he would pay thirty-five to one. Crowell went over and bought the tickets while we watched the jockeys ride around once more and then go out under the trees to the track and gallop slowly up to the turn where the start was to be.

We went up in the grand-stand to watch the race. They had no elastic barrier at San Siro then and the starter lined up all the horses—they looked very small way up the track—and then sent them off with a crack of his long whip. They came past us with the black horse well in front and on the turn he was running away from the others. I watched them on the far side with the glasses and saw the jockey fighting to hold him in, but he could not hold him and when they came around the turn and into the stretch the black horse was fifteen lengths ahead of the others. He went way on up and around the turn after the finish.

"Isn't it wonderful," Catherine said. "We'll have over three thousand lire. He must be a splendid horse."

"I hope his color doesn't run," Crowell said, "before they pay off."

"He was really a lovely horse," Catherine said. "I wonder if Mr Meyers backed him."

"Did you have the winner?" I called to Meyers. He nodded.

Back from the Races, Jack B. Yeats

"I didn't," Mrs Meyers said. "Who did you children bet on?"

"Japalac."

"Really? He's thirty-five to one!"

"We liked his color."

"I didn't. I thought he looked seedy. They told me not to back him."

"He won't pay much," Meyers said.

"He's marked thirty-five to one in the quotes," I said.

"He won't pay much. At the last minute," Meyers said, "they put a lot of money on him."

"Who?"

"Kempton and the boys. You'll see. He won't pay two to one."

"Then we won't get three thousand lire," Catherine said. "I don't like this crooked racing!"

"We'll get two hundred lire."

"That's nothing. That doesn't do us any good. I thought we were going to get three thousand."

"It's crooked and disgusting," Ferguson said.

"Of course," said Catherine, "if it hadn't been crooked we'd never have backed him at all. But I would have liked the three thousand lire."

"Let's go down and get a drink and see what they pay," Crowell said. We went out to where they posted the numbers and the bell rang to pay off and they put up 18.50 after Japalac to win. That meant he paid less then even money on a ten-lire bet.

The Finish

Sir Alfred Munnings

The last two horses I painted in Newmarket were Hyperion and Fairway. Hyperion had then been at stud— was it three or four years? I wonder if Hyperion was the smallest horse that won a Derby. Already I seem to have written a lot about painting winners. Here was a winner that had obtained fame at that time—he was already getting many winners and, I believe, topped the list of winning sires; but let the artist speak for awhile, and forget racing and breeding.

The stud-farm where Hyperion and Fairway dwelt in adjoining boxes, if it were advertised in a journal read by horses might be described as a large two-roomed flat, on the ground-floor, in ideal surroundings. No other two horses were housed better or were in the care of better attendants. Chinery, a heavy man of medium height, full red face, with big arms and thick calves, which always looked as though they were bursting out of their leggings, was Hyperion's groom. Cain (I then called them Cain and Abel), a shorter and more wiry man, with a thinner face and a hooked nose, and of smaller dimensions, was Fairway's groom.

Lord Derby had commissioned me to paint Hyperion, the stallion of the day, and I began with him. I asked myself the question, Why should not this be my supreme effort? I had a store of twenty-four by twenty-inch, three-ply mahogany boards, primed with a semi-absorbent white. On this surface I could paint quickly. What a blessing it is to have a nice-looking stallion to paint, to be able to have him out morning and afternoon, knowing that he is not getting bored—on the contrary, that he may be enjoying it! It brings a change of life into his almost solitary existence. Hyperion was a beautiful little horse, not an Araby head; but he was far beyond the average horse in intelligence. Chinery, his man, adored him, and looked upon him as a brother, although when holding forth on life at the stud he remarked that "when the season was goin' full split, darned if it didn't get on yer nerves—nothing but servin' those blessed mares mornin', noon and night, week in, week out; it's a terrible business!"

Now to come to the painting; for, after all, that was why I went to the stud-farm every morning in one of Chilcott's cars.

I cannot believe, as I sit here writing to-day, that I ever was so full of determination and energy to attain my object. Days went far too quickly; there were days of rain in between. Many an evening have I returned to my friend's in Station Road and said:

"This weather will be the end of me."

A weather-glass hung on the right of the front door in his hall. Always hoping that the wireless and forecasts might be wrong, I tapped that glass before going to bed and when I came down in the morning. I began the horse in sunlight, and as this was to be the horse-portrait of my life, I needed sunlight. An artist can always make use of grey days. I painted Hyperion in his box—a box far larger than many Chelsea studios. I painted his neighbour, Fairway, in his box—a beautiful dark-brown horse. No sooner did I become entangled in the tones of a horse in his box, than out came the sun. I believe that I did say, "Oh, damn the sun!" May I be struck dead for saying such a thing! The sun is life. How well I see that firm, rounded form of Chinery's, with his Rowlandson-like breeches and swelling calves—all true horse-keepers walk out of Rowlandson's pictures—his rubicund face under the sun, his big, bared fore-arms holding the horse.

"Get his quarters a little more to me, Chinery. Whoa! that's all right," I'd say. Chinery all the time using a long spray—I think it was elder—to keep the flies off.

There is a certain depth and transparency in a well-groomed coat of a horse—bay, brown or chestnut. There is nothing opaque about it, neither is there on a bottle or a piece of glazed pottery. On the surface of a live animal, be it a dog, a horse, a cow, a bird, or even a fish out of water, there are high lights, and when we grasp the meaning of these high lights it becomes interesting. We will take the covering of horses. On browns the lights are cooler, greyer—bluer, if you like; on a bay, less cool; on a chestnut inclining to pinky-grey. On a well-grown horse in the sun these lights are devastating. Art writers, full of conceit, empty of vision, their minds urbanized, jeer at my "shiny horses", as they call them. They are quite welcome to their Matisse women—to their Braques, Modiglianis and surrealist horses; their outlook is as queer as that of their fancy artists. What would old Chinery or Cain think of their pet pictures?

I was speaking of the difficulties and troubles of horse-painting, which are a hundredfold. A horse never keeps his ears still. A horse at attention, when he is looking at an object, pricks his ears. Strange as it may seem, he may be aware of what is ahead of or around him, but if ever he looks at an object he pricks his ears. But it is reckoned that a camera can do all this: can give a representation of anything—even of a horse pricking his ears. How often have I stood or sat, my study nearing its completion, holding a particular brush, watching those ears, as a horse gazed at something afar off. I watch; there is no hurry; I am mentally painting the stroke—the horse still looking at whatever it is. I hold my hand—looking at the ear; then I make my stroke. . . .

One day I said to Chinery, "Why can't we take the horse out of his own paddock? He is standing here and dozing."

"Right," said Chinery, "we'll take him through the yard out into that big empty paddock."

I almost wished I had never spoken. With Cain in attendance, box, easel, canvas and all, we moved into the new demesne. The moment Hyperion found himself there he was all alive. He began to haul the sixteen-stone Chinery across the field, moving slowly backwards, his head outstretched, taking Chinery with him on the end of the lead. It was no use Chinery planting his feet and sticking in his heels; he was quietly and steadily pulled to the farther end of the field. Calling for help to Cain, his friend and partner appeared and got behind the horse, finally persuading Hyperion back to where we wanted him. Here we were in a wide, empty paddock; more paddocks, mares and foals in the distance—things for the horse to gaze at afresh.

"Why didn't we do this before, Chinery?" I asked.

"I'm sure I don't know, Sir," was the reply; "there's no reason why he shouldn't stand here now he's watching those mares over there."

Little does Chinery know what is going on in my own mind. I am concentrating on a mere study of a horse painted upon a twenty-four-by-twenty board. I am still wondering what is the actual colour of the shadow on the horse. But no writing can give any idea of the intricacies, the colour, tones, knowledge of horse anatomy, conglomerated together in the mind of one who is trying to paint a horse. I often think, when looking at an old horse-picture, that the artist had been up against the same problems. For all that, there is no reason why we should not go on. The curse of human nature with regard to the Arts is Progress—always Progress. By all means let us

Portrait of Lord Derby's Hyperion (another version), Sir Alfred Munnings

have our wireless, our electricity, our Calor gas. Art is of the mind—a different thing. Art is—or should be—part of life. It balances up our primitive instincts. Painting, sculpture, writing, music come from the brain—from the soul. To take suddenly a cynical turn—to make a somersault—to strike out in what one thinks is a new fashion, could not be the choice or intention of a normal mind. There is no time in life for him who is dealing with Nature's truths to turn to stunts. After all, a stunt may only be a cloak to hide a man's incapacity.

These digressions carry me no farther, so let me get back to Hyperion in his new surroundings. I have talked about painting a horse's ears. What of his eyes? What of the modelling of his head—of his neck, where the most puzzling things happen in the way of lighting? But enough of all this! As the last thing, let us take a horse's tail! Hyperion carried his like an Arab's. It was thick, with a slight wave; when not in movement, drooping to his quarters, the longest hairs touched the ground. How is a man to paint such a tail? There it is; you have only to move the horse and he holds it out. When the tail of an ungroomed colt at grass is lit by the sun it shines, but the tail of a well-attended horse such as Hyperion, or any racehorse, glistens with health and well-being. All

[78]

I can say is—let him who can, paint it. I give up; I can no more explain these painting problems than I could dart like a chaffinch with a striped wing from one tree to another. It is easier to talk of the stud, the big barn, the buildings, or to tell of the conversations between Chinery and his mate, Cain.

Sketch for an Equestrian Statue, Leonardo da Vinci

The Story of Mill Reef

John Oaksey

Mill Reef went back to the downs only twice more before Derby Day. Philip Waldron rode him a mile tucked in behind Winter Fair on 26 May and three days later, four days before the race itself, he came five furlongs sharp up the undulating "Monday morning" gallop.

The zest and fire with which he moved that day gladdened Ian Balding's heart, but nothing could set his mind altogether at rest. The horse had done everything asked of him, but had enough—or perhaps too much—been asked? That is the trainer's eternal dilemma, and the trainer of an Epsom Derby favourite has other worries besides.

Horse Races, Gustave Doré

Security is one of them and by this time, the block of boxes where Mill Reef lived had already been fitted with burglar alarms. To make assurance doubly sure, an off-duty policeman, complete with a small but pugnacious terrier, kept watch at night and when the horsebox left for Epsom it was preceded by a Securicor van containing two armed guards. Considerable pressure had been put on Ian Balding to travel the horse a day earlier so that he could spend the last night in the heavily guarded racecourse stables. But remembering Mill Reef's nervous state before the Guineas the trainer stuck to his guns. The horsebox left early on 2 June, 1971, and that was just as well, for as anyone who went to the Derby that sweltering day remembers all too clearly, the whole Epsom area was one vast traffic jam from midday onwards.

Ian Balding, who had Winter Fair to saddle in the race before the Derby, was among those inextricably bogged down within two miles of the course and had to run for it, top hat and all,

Man O'War at Belmont Park, 1919, Franklin B. Voss

[81]

leaving Emma and his mother-in-law to do the best they could. By that time Mill Reef had long been secure in the racecourse stables, whiling away the time by tapping his forefeet against the concrete door frame. His own box at Kingsclere had been given a special "Tartan" surface like an Olympic running track and John Hallum thinks that the different feel and sound of the concrete amused and interested him. However that may be, he managed to knock both front shoes out of place and Tom Reilly had to replate him before he left for the paddock. There, cool, elegant and untroubled by the thronging crowds, he added a badly needed touch of class to what was by common consent a somewhat undistinguished-looking field.

"Until he entered the Parade Ring," Roger Mortimer wrote, "one got the impression that the drab uniformity of the classless society had spread to the equine world."

To those who had not seen him since Newmarket, Mill Reef had clearly put on weight and muscle and although two small patches of sweat appeared on his flanks just before he was saddled, they vanished before the Parade.

The going at Epsom was as near perfect as makes no difference and, cantering past the stands, Mill Reef would surely have cut any daisies that happened to be growing there. He always gallops with his head and neck well stretched and Geoff Lewis always rode him on a longer than average rein. On Derby Day, I remember noting anxiously that he seemed to be pulling harder than usual, but Geoff thinks this impression was due to the slight remaining weakness in his own hands. And in any case, leaving nothing to chance, Ian Balding had stationed a senior stable-lad called Paddy Heffernan (who had come to Epsom with Winter Fair) down in the paddock just in case Mill Reef should arrive there going too fast. In fact, he pulled up calmly enough and Paddy accompanied him across the road and down the narrow crowd-lined gangway which leads up to the Derby start.

Meanwhile, to the unkind amusement of some and the despair of others, the much-fancied French colt Bourbon had lost both his temper, his bridle and, for a while, his jockey in front of the stands. The blinkers which had galvanized Bourbon in the Prix Hocquart now appeared to madden him and although the Clerk of the Course, Major Peter Beckwith-Smith, was able (to his eternal credit) to conjure up a spare bridle, it still took the combined efforts of Bourbon's trainer, Alec Head, his son Freddy and a cooperative mounted policeman to get the recalcitrant colt back past the stands. By the time he arrived at the start, needless to say, Bourbon's chances had evaporated in a cloud of steam and wasted energy. (Poor Freddy Head cannot have the happiest memories of Epsom, for the following year, Lyphard carried him so wide round Tattenham Corner that, according to an uncharitable rival jockey, "the gypsies in the fairground were asking for danger money".) Bourbon's antics, in fact, served one useful purpose because, but for them, Priscilla Hastings and Emma Balding would have missed the Derby. It was only as Mr Alec Marsh got the field away (four minutes late) that they arrived, hot and panting, in the stands. There followed, at least for them and Mill Reef's other supporters, the sort of race that usually happens only in one's dreams.

They went, for the first three sharply uphill furlongs, only at a moderate gallop. Linden Tree, blinkered for the first time and pulling hard, was up in front with Credit Man, whose rider, Yves Saint Martin, was, as a matter of interest, to make the early running in three successive Epsom Derby rides.

In those first two furlongs, as the film shows, Mill Reef was tossing his head impatiently against the bit and looked, for a moment, like pulling his way undesirably close to the leaders. But Geoff quickly covered him up behind Beaming Lee and Credit Man and, by the top of Tattenham Hill where Linden Tree had gone a length clear in front, the favourite was tucked in sixth or seventh, three horses off the inside rail.

The Fallen Jockey, Edgar Degas

It is here—down the hill to Tattenham Corner—that most hard luck stories are born in the Derby. About half the runners are already either beaten or at full stretch and, to a jockey coming from behind, they represent a field of floating mines in which his chances can all too easily be blown sky high.

Now, halfway down the hill, Geoff Lewis had one such hazard to negotiate. He had always hoped to track Joe Mercer and Homeric into the straight, partly because Joe could be relied on better than most to keep his horse balanced and partly because, on his Lingfield form, Homeric seemed reasonably sure to be somewhere near the leaders. Both assumptions proved correct but now, with Homeric outside him and half a length ahead, Geoff saw Credit Man begin to falter and fall back slap in Mill Reef's path.

A picture taken only seconds later at Tattenham Corner shows how completely the Irish colt collapsed, for in it he has only three behind him. That is what I mean by floating mines and, to avoid this one, Geoff desperately needed a yard or so of elbow-room. Joe Mercer had every right, in theory, to deny him and could have done so without the slightest danger to himself or Homeric. There are some jockeys of whom, as Geoff says, "You'd as soon call for room as ask Scrooge for

The Duke of Devonshire's Flying Childers, 1740, James Seymour

a quid," but Joe Mercer is not one of them. Now, hearing Geoff's urgent shout, he edged Homeric out a fraction and, with Credit Man hanging the other way, a providential gap appeared.

To take it, however, Mill Reef had to quicken sharply and the next few seconds confirmed the truth that an ideal Derby colt needs many of the characteristics of a top class polo pony. For, having darted outside Credit Man, Geoff was able to ease back in again behind Homeric in half a dozen strides. Seen on film, it is a memorable display of handiness and, as a result of it, swinging down into Tattenham Corner, Mill Reef was poised ideally in fourth place with only Linden Tree, Lombardo and Homeric between him and the winning post.

There were, of course, more than three furlongs still to go, but in the twenty-odd Derbys I have watched, I do not remember one in which the result was more predictable so far from home. Linden Tree was still going strong and so for another furlong was Lombardo. But every line of Geoff Lewis's body shouted confidence and with all his three rivals at full stretch, Mill Reef was cruising on the bit.

He did not win like that, though, and, to the very short list of horses who ever fully extended him, the gallant Linden Tree's name must now be added. For a moment, two furlongs out, Linden Tree himself looked sure to be passed by Lombardo and he had only just repelled that challenge, when Mill Reef sailed up the middle of the course to join him. To us in the stands it looked all over, but Duncan Keith did not think so, nor did Linden Tree. With nearly a furlong left, Geoff had to pull his whip through on Mill Reef and ring urgently for full speed ahead. The response was immediate and decisive but Geoff did not stop riding and the two lengths by which he won could not, I think, have been very much increased. Poor Linden Tree: this desperate struggle was, as it turned out, his final bow, for three weeks later in the Irish Derby, he refused to race at all. But on 2 June 1971 he was a very good three-year-old indeed, good enough, one might guess, to win at least six Derbys out of ten.

Behind him now, Lombardo clearly failed to stay, Homeric could not quicken and, past them both came Irish Ball, the only horse in the race who could in any sense of the word be called "unlucky".

Irish Ball's chief misfortune was that Lester Piggott, who could have ridden him, chose The Parson instead. For having, by his own account, got into all sorts of trouble down the hill, the French jockey A. Gilbert proceeded up the straight to give a lifelike imitation of an over-excited windmill. His antics sent poor Irish Ball rolling first this way then that and in the end, it was an heroic achievement on the horse's part to finish third. On the Curragh, a course much better suited to Monsieur Gilbert's methods, Irish Ball was later to slam Lombardo and he also ran a courageous second in the Washington D.C. International to Mill Reef's childhood friend, Run The Gauntlet.

Geoff Lewis had one more moment of anxiety on Derby Day, for Linden Tree (and who shall blame him?) threatened to lash out as Mill Reef passed behind him after pulling up. The broadest, happiest grin on Epsom Downs vanished for an instant from Geoff's face, but all was well.

So back they came in triumph—greeted first by a speechless John Hallum, then by Bill Jennings and Paddy Heffernan and, a close fourth by Dai Davies, the cheerful, tireless Welshman whose exhausting job is to relay via the Press Association the news of great events like this as near as possible before they happen. To Dai, Paul Mellon described it as "the happiest day of my life", and John Hallum felt the same. Of all the great memories Mill Reef left him, this comes first.

"To do a Derby winner"—he says—"No lad can ever ask for more than that."

That evening, when Mill Reef's horsebox got back to Kingsclere, the village was *en fête*. Flags and bunting hung across the road and a happy crowd had gathered at the turning off towards

[85]

Park House. "They wanted us to get him out there," John Hallum recalls, "and when we wouldn't they ran behind us all the way home."

At last Mill Reef unboxed in triumph and, for half an hour, walked graciously among his fans in front of a row of cottages which have ever since been named after him. It had been a long hard day but if he was tired it did not show. Patted and stroked from head to tail, he remained as calm and unflustered as he and Geoff Lewis had been throughout the Derby.

FROM

The Staig's Boy William

Fred Urquhart

William's birthday, 12 July, 1765, was one of a two-day meeting at Newmarket, and he was near the winning-post when Lord Bolingbroke's dark grey horse Gimcrack won the main event.

A few days after that William and Mr Garrick were walking near the Rubbing House when they saw a gentleman standing in front of an easel painting a picture of the grey. Gimcrack's head was being held by a man wearing a tricorn hat and knee breeches. A bare headed groom knelt almost under the horse, doing something to one of his back hoofs. William and Mr Garrick stood to watch. The artist, a middle aged stoutish gentleman in a white powdered wig and a brown coat that bore many snuff and paint stains, frowned when the boy and the cat came and stood at his elbow, then, suddenly aware of their beauty, he smiled and said, "Watch for as long as it pleases you, boy, but stand not quite so close, I pray you. I must have elbow room."

William, who seldom paid heed to requests or commands, unless they were couched in violent terms and accompanied perhaps by blows, stepped back at once. He beamed at the gentleman and stood still, watching every stroke of the brush. Mr Garrick, after one loud introductory miaow, became silent. With this strange but apparently appreciative audience the artist painted on for some time, passing occasional remarks to the horse's attendants. Then he told the groom he could stand up. "I shall need you to return to that pose later, my good fellow," he said. "But no more today. Your knees must be sore. Off with you!"

The groom was protesting that he had no wish to leave the horse until he led him back to the stable, giving voluble reasons for this, when he stopped in the midst of them to pull his forelock. Lord Bolingbroke and Sir Henry Wedderburn, escorting a beautiful young lady, had come up unnoticed.

The artist smiled at the lady, who was attired in a mauve dress and a large flat white leghorn hat decorated with mauve and white flowers. "Your obedient, Lady Sarah," he said, bowing. "Your obedient, gentlemen."

[86]

A Dash for the Timber, Frederic Remington

Cowboys Roping a Bear, James Walker

"La, Mr Stubbs, what a delight to meet you here," Lady Sarah said, giving him her hand to kiss. "And to find you painting Gimcrack. Is he not the sweetest little horse."

She patted the grey's neck. William gazed at her, his mouth open. He had never seen such a lovely lady. "Well, William, are you studying art?" Sir Henry said, gently ruffling the boy's hair. "And is Toby Garrick wishful to be an artist too?"

"What a beautiful boy!" Lady Sarah cried. "Is he yours, Harry?"

She advanced towards William, putting out her hand to touch his cheek, but Sir Henry grasped her wrist, preventing her. "The cat, my love," he warned. "'Tis a fearsome creature and guards William most jealously. I would not wish your hands to suffer from his claws."

Mr Garrick opened his mouth wide and gave a fearful wail; then he jumped from William's arms and, tail high, he sidled towards Lady Sarah and rubbed himself ingratiatingly against her skirt. She was about to stoop and pet him, but stopped. She looked at Sir Henry and laughed.

Lord Bolingbroke, who had been peering at the painting through his quizzing glass, said good humouredly, "I thought m'jockey was to be in the picture, Mr Stubbs. Payin' you all that money, I expect a crowded canvas!"

"He will be, m'Lord." The artist's eyes twinkled. "He will be when 'tis finished, as agreed. He was here a while back, but as he was merely cooling his heels I sent him off on his business. I have no use for him until tomorrow or the next day. See, I have left this space on the canvas for his likeness, to Gimcrack's rear."

"Let us hope then that Gimcrack does not take umbrage and lash out at him with his heels before the painting is finished," Bolingbroke said. "Or before his next race. I depend on this jockey to make m'horse win."

"When will his next race be, Boley?" Lady Sarah asked.

"He is committed to run in a King's Plate at Doncaster at the end of this season. Between this and then I know not."

Sir Henry said, "I would be honoured, Mr Stubbs, if you would do a painting of my champion Challenger. He has never been beaten, and I wish him to be celebrated on canvas."

"Sir Henry, I would be vastly pleased to comply with your wish," Mr Stubbs said. "But, alas, I have so many commissions this season that I very much doubt if I shall be able to fulfil most of them. I was forced even to refuse his Royal Highness of Cumberland when he asked me shortly before he died if I would paint his chestnut yearling Eclipse. His Highness was displeased, but no matter, I cannot undertake commissions I cannot fulfil."

"I hear Eclipse has been sold to a grazier or a meat salesman or some such who rejoices in the name of Mr Wildman," Lord Bolingbroke said. "For seventy-five pounds. I would have given more."

"'Tis said that Eclipse is likely to become a winner," Sir Henry said lazily. "Cumberland thought very highly of him. I'll wager, though, that he'll never be as good as my Challenger."

"And I'll wager he'll never be as good as my brave little Gimcrack," Bolingbroke cut in.

"Challenger is unbeaten."

"So is Gimcrack."

"La, my dears!" Lady Sarah said languidly. "You men are so tedious when you speak of horses. You are just like my husband. Sir Charles thinks more of horses and their paces than he thinks of his wife, poor soul, and hers."

"My dear Sarah," Bolingbroke said. "If you will permit me to say so, Bunbury is a blind idiot not to cherish you more."

"These are kind words, Boley," the lady said. "But I feel they are wasted on the desert air. Bunbury knows not of my existence."

[87]

Sir Henry coughed and said, "Mr Stubbs, would you be prepared to paint Challenger at some later date? Even if, perchance, it is when his racing is over and he has been put to stud?"

"I shall be delighted, sir," the artist said. "As soon as I have completed my book on the anatomy of the horse I will be much freer to fulfil commissions."

"I can see the painting already," Sir Henry said dreamily. "Challenger, the unbeaten champion . . ."

"How can you say that, Harry, when he has never raced against Gimcrack?" Bolingbroke cried angrily. "I'll wager that if they were matched, my horse would win by lengths."

"I doubt it. Both are grandsons of the Godolphin Arabian, and though Challenger is a year the older I think he would outmatch your horse in both speed and stamina."

"What will you wager me, Harry?"

"I will wager nothing," Sir Henry said lazily. "I give you my honest opinion. I will not bet on it."

Gimcrack on Newmarket Heath, George Stubbs

[88]

Hunter Trials

John Betjeman

It's awf'lly bad luck on Diana,
   Her ponies have swallowed their bits;
She fished down their throats with a spanner
   And frightened them all into fits.

So now she's attempting to borrow.
   Do lend her some bits, Mummy, *do*;
I'll lend her my own for tomorrow,
   But today I'll be wanting them too.

Just look at Prunella on Guzzle,
   The wizardest pony on earth;
Why doesn't she slacken his muzzle
   And tighten the breech in his girth?

I say, Mummy, there's Mrs Geyser
   And doesn't she look pretty sick?
I bet it's because Mona Lisa
   Was hit on the hock with a brick.

Miss Blewitt says Monica threw it,
   But Monica says it was Joan,
And Joan's very thick with Miss Blewitt,
   So Monica's sulking alone.

And Margaret failed in her paces,
   Her withers got tied in a noose,
So her coronets caught in the traces
   And now all her fetlocks are loose.

Oh, it's me now. I'm terribly nervous.
   I wonder if Smudges will shy.
She's practically certain to swerve as
   Her Pelham is over one eye.

Oh wasn't it naughty of Smudges?
　Oh, Mummy, I'm sick with disgust.
She threw me in front of the Judges,
　And my silly old collarbone's bust.

Willowbrook Show, Norman Thelwell

FROM

"Plain or Ringlets?"

R. S. Surtees

Tallyho! There's a holloa at the low end of the wood, and Jock getting Galashiels by the head, crams away to the place. All right! He's gone!

　　　　"Hark! what loud shouts
Re-echo thro' the grove! He breaks away!
Shrill horns proclaim his flight. Each straggling hound
Strains o'er the lawn to reach the distant pack;
'Tis triumph all, and joy."

Not all joy, perhaps, though we dare say it would have been in Somerville's time when he wrote the above lines. Already the vision of Thorneyburn Brook and Butterlow fences arise in the minds of those who do not like bathing or bullfinching. Still it is a case of do all you can, and

"dream the rest,"

and each man elbows and legs himself out of cover, resolved to see as much as he can. Prince, Peers, peasants, all mixed up in heterogeneous confusion. The "get away" from a fox cover is the real leveller of rank, far more efficacious than any Reform bill.

We are sorry we cannot accompany the horsemen in their flight over Longhope Hill and down into the Hewish Vale, tell how the war-horse stopped with the Prince at Muddiford Pond, and Lord Marchhare sending his chestnut at some impracticable palings, lighted on his head, and knocked his hat-crown out. How the Duke of Tergiversation thought he had had enough at Snowden Mill, and Archy Ellenger at Harper's Green. How the field gradually tailed off, and Galashiels gradually gave in till Haggish deserted him at farmer Muttons, and finished the run on foot—"who-hooping" the fox at Toddlewood Hill. All this we must leave, to return to our hero Mr Bunting in Sunnyside Wood.

The rides there were very deep and holding, well calculated to take the fiery edge off even the most sportive tailed horse, let alone one that could hardly go on the road, and Owen Ashford's distress was painfully apparent to every one except his rider. Mr Bunting thought it must be want of work, which would most likely go off after a gallop. So he just jogged him up and down the rides with the rest of the field, the cry of the hounds animating the horse into extra exertion. But nature will not be said nay to, and ere the grand *Tallyho!* Owen Ashford had done his "*possible*", finished before he had well begun. Nevertheless, Mr Bunting held him on, hoping he might get the second wind peculiar to well-bred horses. Perhaps he might be better in the open. So he took his turn at the lower of the two gaps in the ragged wood-fence leading out of the cover, and with a desperate effort planted the gallant grey in the middle of it. There he stood coughing, and wheezing, and rocking-horsing, unable to get either backwards or forwards. The horsemen

The Hunt, John Leech

Hunting Scene, George Morland

behind him then took the other gap, and in this undignified position our friend was doomed to see the last of the field. Presently Billingford, the woodman, came panting up, and, advising Mr Bunting to dismount, applied his brawny shoulder to the horse's quarters, and fairly thrust him over into the next field.

"He must be bad, surely!" exclaimed Billingford, as the horse lay heaving and gasping like one of Mr Rarey's "Incorrigibles", after a lesson, a very different looking animal indeed to what he was in Sligo Mews.

"I think he must," replied Mr Bunting, wondering what Captain Cavendish Chichester would say if he killed him.

"I'd get him up, and get him into the house, if I was you," observed the woodman.

"Well, I think that would be the best thing," replied our hero, "only the question is, how to do it."

"He heaves heavily," observed the man, eyeing Owen Ashford's flank, "wish he mayn't have got the staggers." Most people have some pet disease with which they invest every horse that is ill.

Just then Owen Ashford raised his head, and after staring about him with a fixed unmeaning glare, he got first on his hind-quarters, and then after a rabbit-like sit, with a desperate grunt, raised himself wholly on all fours. There he stood more like the wooden horse in a saddler's shop than anything likely to go.

"He's surely been very sair ridden that hus," observed Billingford, eyeing his distended nostrils suspiciously.

"Not a bit of it," replied Mr Bunting, "He's hardly been out of a walk."

"Then he mun be very bad somehow," rejoined the man, "I would get him home, gin I ware you."

"I wish I had him home," replied Mr Bunting, eyeing the horse's rigid frame.

"I'd slack his girths a bit, sir, I'd slack his girths," observed the man, still conning Owen over.

Mr Bunting did slack his girths, and the horse appeared relieved by the operation, after a good cough, wheeze, grunt, he dropped his head, and began to nibble at the grass by the rail side. That was encouraging, and after getting his bearings from the man and inquiring where he would find a veterinary surgeon, Mr Bunting gave Billingford a shilling for his trouble; and horse in hand, set out to work his way homewards on foot, to the great disadvantage of his boots.

Poor Owen was very weak and tottering at first, and went coughing and grunting, and sobbing as though he would break his heart; but he gradually picked up when he got upon the hard road, so much so indeed, that, after rising Little Hay Hill again, Mr Bunting, tired of walking, and feeling for his "Bartleys", inveigled the horse alongside a field-gate, when drawing his girths, he deposited himself very gently in the saddle, and then proceeded at a foot's pace along the green strip by the side of the road. And with grunts and groans and occasional stoppages to stare, poor Owen Ashford at length began to go not so far amiss, though the country-people who saw him all thought the Duke's hounds must have had a terrible run.

St Valentine's Day

Wilfrid Scawen Blunt

Today, all day, I rode upon the down,
With hounds and horsemen, a brave company.
On this side in its glory lay the sea,
On that the Sussex Weald, a sea of brown.
The wind was light, and brightly the sun shone,
And still we gallop'd on from gorse to gorse:

And once, when check'd, a thrush sang, and my horse
Prick'd his quick ears as to a sound unknown.
    I knew the Spring was come. I knew it even
Better than all by this, that through my chase
In bush and stone and hill and sea and heaven
I seem'd to see and follow still your face.
Your face my quarry was. For it I rode,
My horse a thing of wings, myself a god.

Captain John Parkhurst of Catesby Abbey, Northamptonshire, Sawrey Gilpin

The Maltese Cat

Rudyard Kipling

They had good reason to be proud, and better reason to be afraid, all twelve of them; for, though they had fought their way, game by game, up the teams entered for the polo tournament, they were meeting the Archangels that afternoon in the final match; and the Archangels' men were playing with half-a-dozen ponies apiece. As the game was divided into six quarters of eight minutes each, that meant a fresh pony after every halt. The Skidars' team, even supposing there were no accidents, could only supply one pony for every other change; and two to one is heavy odds. Again, as Shiraz, the grey Syrian, pointed out, they were meeting the pink and pick of the polo ponies of Upper India; ponies that had cost from a thousand rupees each, while they themselves were a cheap lot gathered, often from country carts, by their masters who belonged to a poor but honest native infantry regiment.

"Money means pace and weight," said Shiraz, rubbing his black silk nose dolefully along his neat-fitting boot, "and by the maxims of the game as I know it—"

"Ah, but we aren't playing the maxims," said the Maltese Cat. "We're playing the game, and we've the great advantage of knowing the game. Just think a stride, Shiraz. We've pulled up from bottom to second place in two weeks against all those fellows on the ground here; and that's because we play with our heads as well as our feet."

"It makes me feel undersized and unhappy all the same," said Kittiwynk, a mouse-coloured mare with a red browband and the cleanest pair of legs that ever an aged pony owned. "They're twice our size . . ."

Kittiwynk looked at the gathering and sighed. The hard, dusty Umballa polo-ground was lined with thousands of soldiers, black and white, not counting hundreds and hundreds of carriages, and drags, and dog-carts, and ladies with brilliant-coloured parasols, and officers in uniform and out of it, and crowds of natives behind them; and orderlies on camels who had halted to watch the game, instead of carrying letters up and down the station, and native horse-dealers running about on thin-eared Biluchi mares, looking for a chance to sell a few first-class polo ponies. Then there were the ponies of thirty teams that entered for the Upper India Free-For-All-Cup—nearly every pony of worth and dignity from Mhow to Peshawar, from Allahabad to Multan; prize ponies, Arabs, Syrian, Barb, country bred, Deccanee, Waziri, and Kabul ponies of every colour and shape and temper that you could imagine. Some of them were in mat-roofed stables close to the polo-ground, but most were under saddle while their masters, who had been defeated in the earlier games, trotted in and out and told each other exactly how the game should be played.

It was a glorious sight, and the come-and-go of the quick hoofs, and the incessant salutations of ponies that had met before on other polo-grounds or racecourses were enough to drive a four-

A Game of Polo, Isfahan, *c.* 1600

footed thing wild.

But the Skidars' team were careful not to know their neighbours, though half the ponies on the ground were anxious to scrape acquaintance with the little fellows that had come from the North, and, so far, had swept the board.

"Let's see," said a soft, golden-coloured Arab, who had been playing very badly the day before, to the Maltese Cat, "didn't we meet in Abdul Rahman's stable in Bombay four seasons ago? I won the Paikpattan Cup next season, you may remember."

"Not me," said the Maltese Cat politely. "I was at Malta then, pulling a vegetable cart. I don't race. I play the game."

"O-oh!" said the Arab, cocking his tail and swaggering off.

"Keep yourselves to yourselves," said the Maltese Cat to his companions. "We don't want to rub noses with all those goose-rumped half-breeds of Upper India. When we've won this cup they'll give their shoes to know us."

"*We* shan't win the cup," said Shiraz. "How do you feel?"

"Stale as last night's feed when a musk-rat has run over it," said Polaris, a rather heavy-shouldered grey, and the rest of the team agreed with him.

"The sooner you forget that the better," said the Maltese Cat cheerfully. "They've finished tiffin in the big tent. We shall be wanted now. If your saddles are not comfy, kick. If your bits aren't easy, rear, and let the *saises* know whether your boots are tight."

Each pony had his *sais*, his groom, who lived and ate and slept with the pony, and had betted a great deal more than he could afford on the result of the game. There was no chance of anything going wrong, and, to make sure each *sais* was shampooing the legs of his pony to the last minute. Behind the *saises* sat as many of the Skidars' regiment as had leave to attend the match—about half the native officers, and a hundred or two dark, black-bearded men with the regimental pipers nervously fingering the big be-ribboned bagpipes. The Skidars were what they call a Pioneer regiment; and the bagpipes made the national music of half the men. The native officers held bundles of polo-sticks, long cane-handled mallets, and as the grandstand filled after lunch they arranged themselves by ones and twos at different points round the ground, so that if a stick were broken the player would not have far to ride for a new one. An impatient British cavalry band struck up "If you want to know the time, ask a p'leeceman!" and the two umpires in light dust-coats danced out on two little excited ponies. The four players of the Archangels' team followed, and the sight of their beautiful mounts made Shiraz groan again.

"Wait till we know," said the Maltese Cat. "Two of 'em are playing in blinkers, and that means they can't see to get out of the way of their own side, or they *may* shy at the umpires' ponies. They've *all* got white web reins that are sure to stretch or slip!"

"And," said Kittiwynk, dancing to take the stiffness out of her, "they carry their whips in their hands instead of on their wrists, Hah!"

"True enough. No man can manage his stick and his reins, and his whip that way," said the Maltese Cat. "I've fallen over every square yard of the Malta ground, and I ought to know." He quivered his little flea-bitten withers just to show how satisfied he felt; but his heart was not so light. Ever since he had drifted into India on a troopship, taken, with an old rifle, as part payment for a racing debt, the Maltese Cat had played and preached polo to the Skidars' team on the Skidars' stony polo-ground. Now a polo-pony is like a poet. If he is born with a love for the game he can be made. The Maltese Cat knew that bamboos grew solely in order that polo-balls might be turned from their roots, that grain was given to ponies to keep them in hard condition and that ponies were shod to prevent them slipping on a turn. But, besides all these things, he knew every trick and device of the finest game of the world, and for two seasons he had been teaching the others all he knew or guessed.

"Remember," he said for the hundredth time as the riders came up, "we *must* play together, and you *must* play with your heads. Whatever happens, follow the ball. Who goes out first?"

Kittiwynk, Shiraz, Polaris, and a short high little bay fellow with tremendous hocks and no withers worth speaking of (he was called Corks) were being girthed up, and the soldiers in the background stared with all their eyes.

"I want you men to keep quiet," said Lutyens, the captain of the team, "and especially *not* to blow your pipes."

"Not if we win, Captain Sahib?" asked a piper.

"If we win, you can do what you please," said Lutyens, with a smile, as he slipped the loop of his stick over his wrist, and wheeled to canter to his place. The Archangels' ponies were a little bit above themselves on account of the many-coloured crowd so close in the ground. Their riders were excellent players, but they were a team of crack players instead of a crack team, and that made all the difference in the world. They honestly meant to play together, but it is very hard for four men, each the best of the team he is picked from, to remember that in polo no brilliancy of hitting or riding makes up for playing alone. Their captain shouted his orders to them by name, and it is a curious thing that if you call his name aloud in public after an Englishman you make him hot and fretty. Lutyens said nothing to his men because it had all been said before. He pulled up Shiraz for he was playing "back", to guard the goal. Powell on Polaris was half-back, and Macnamara and Hughes on Corks and Kittiwynk were forwards. The tough bamboo-root ball was put into the middle of the ground one hundred and fifty yards from the ends, and Hughes crossed sticks, heads-up with the captain of the Archangels, who saw fit to play forward, and that is a place from which you cannot easily control the team. The little click as the cane-shafts met was heard all over the ground, and then Hughes made some sort of quick wrist-stroke that just dribbled the ball a few yards. Kittiwynk knew that stroke of old, and followed as a cat follows a mouse. While the captain of the Archangels was wrenching his pony round Hughes struck with all his strength, and next instant Kittiwynk was away, Corks followed close behind her, their little feet pattering like rain-drops on glass.

"Pull out to the left," said Kittiwynk between her teeth, "it's coming our way, Corks!"

The back and half-back of the Archangels were tearing down on her just as she was within reach of the ball. Hughes leaned forward with a loose rein, and cut it away to the left almost under Kittiwynk's feet, and it hopped and skipped off to Corks, who saw that, if he were not quick, it would run beyond the boundaries. That long bouncing drive gave the Archangels time to wheel and send three men across the ground to head off Corks. Kittiwynk stayed where she was, for she knew the game. Corks was on the ball half a fraction of a second before the others came up, and Macnamara, with a back-handed stroke, sent it back across the ground to Hughes, who saw the way clear to the Archangels' goal and smacked the ball in before any one quite knew what had happened.

"That's luck," said Corks, as they changed ends. "A goal in three minutes for three hits and no riding to speak of."

"Don't know," said Polaris. "We've made 'em angry too soon. Shouldn't wonder if they try to rush us off our feet next time."

The Archangels came down like a wolf on the fold, for they were tired of football and they wanted polo. They got it more and more. Just after the game began, Lutyens hit a ball that was coming towards him rapidly, and it rose in the air, as a ball sometimes will, with the whirr of a frightened partridge. Shikast heard, but could not see it for the minute, though he looked

A Game of Polo, Li Lin

everywhere and up in the air as the Maltese Cat had taught him. When he saw it ahead and overhead, he went forward with Powell as fast as he could put foot to ground. It was then that Powell, a quiet and level-headed man as a rule, became inspired and played a stroke that sometimes comes off successfully on a quiet afternoon of long practice. He took his stick in both hands, and standing up in his stirrups, swiped at the ball in the air, Munipore fashion. There was one second of paralysed astonishment, and then all four sides of the ground went up in a yell of applause and delight as the ball flew true (you could see the amazed Archangels ducking in their saddles to get out of the line of flight, and looking at it with open mouths), and the regimental pipes of the Skidars squealed from the railings as long as the piper had breath.

Shikast heard the stroke; but he heard the head of the stick fly off at the same time. Nine hundred and ninety-nine ponies out of a thousand would have gone tearing on after the ball with a useless player pulling at their heads, but Powell knew him, and he knew Powell; and the instant he felt Powell's right leg shift a trifle on the saddle-flap he headed to the boundary, where a native officer was frantically waving a new stick. Before the shouts had ended Powell was armed again.

Once before in his life the Maltese Cat had heard that very same stroke played off his own back, and had profited by the confusion it made. This time he acted on experience, and leaving Bamboo to guard the goal in case of accidents, came through the others like a flash, head and tail low, Lutyens standing up to ease him—swept on and on before the other side knew what was the matter, and nearly pitched on his head between the Archangels' goal-post as Lutyens tipped the ball in after a straight scurry of a hundred and fifty yards. If there was one thing more than another upon which the Maltese Cat prided himself it was on the quick, streaking kind of run half across the ground. He did not believe in taking balls round the field unless you were clearly over-matched. After this they gave the Archangels five minutes' football, and an expensive fast pony hates football because it rumples his temper.

Who's Who showed himself even better than Polaris in this game. He did not permit any wriggling away, but bored joyfully into the scrimmage as if he had his nose in a feed-box, and were looking for something nice. Little Shikast jumped on the ball the minute it got clear, and every time an Archangel pony followed it he found Shikast standing over it asking what was the matter.

Polo Player, T'ang dynasty

"If we can live through this quarter," said the Maltese Cat, "I shan't care. Don't take it out of yourselves. Let them do the lathering."

So the ponies as their riders explained afterwards, "shut up". The Archangels kept them tied fast in front of their goal, but it cost the Archangels' ponies all that was left of their tempers; and ponies began to kick, and men began to repeat compliments, and they chopped at the legs of Who's Who, and he set his teeth and stayed where he was, and the dust stood up like a tree over the scrimmage till that hot quarter ended.

They found the ponies very excited and confident when they went to their *saises*; and the Maltese Cat had to warn them that the worst of the game was coming.

"Now *we* are all going in for the second time," said he, "and *they* are trotting out fresh ponies. You'll think you can gallop, but you'll find you can't, and then you'll be sorry."

"But two goals to nothing is a halter-long lead," said Kittiwynk prancing.

"How long does it take to get a goal?" the Maltese Cat answered. "For pity sake, don't run away with the notion that the game is half-won just because we happen to be in luck now. They'll ride you into the grandstand if they can; you must *not* give 'em a chance. Follow the ball."

"Football as usual?" said Polaris. "My hock's half as big as a nose-bag."

"Don't let them have a look at the ball if you can help it. Now leave me alone, I must get all the rest I can before the last quarter."

He hung down his head and let all his muscles go slack, Shikast, Bamboo, and Who's Who copying his example.

"Better not watch the game," he said. "We aren't playing, and we shall only take it out of ourselves if we grow anxious. Look at the ground and pretend it's fly-time."

They did their best, but it was hard advice to follow. The hoofs were drumming and the sticks were rattling all up and down the ground, and yells of applause from the English troops told that the Archangels were pressing the Skidars hard. The native soldiers behind the ponies groaned and grunted, and said things in undertones, and presently they heard a long drawn shout and a clatter of hurrahs!

"One to the Archangels," said Shikast, without raising his head. "Time's nearly up. Oh, my sire and dam!"

"Faiz Ullah," said the Maltese Cat, "if you don't play to the last nail in your shoes this time, I'll kick you on the ground before all the other ponies."

"I'll do my best when my time comes," said the little Arab sturdily.

The *saises* looked at each other gravely as they rubbed their ponies' legs. This was the first time when long purses began to tell, and everybody knew it. Kittiwynk and the others came back with the sweat dripping over their hoofs and their tails telling sad stories.

"They're better than we are," said Shiraz. "I knew how it would be."

"Shut your big head," said the Maltese Cat; "we've one goal to the good yet."

"Yes, but it's two Arabs and two countrybreds to play now," said Corks. "Faiz Ullah, remember!" He spoke in a biting voice.

As Lutyens mounted Grey Dawn he looked at his men, and they did not look pretty. They were covered with dust and sweat in streaks. Their yellow boots were almost black, their wrists were red and lumpy, and their eyes seemed two inches deep in their heads, but the expression in the eyes was satisfactory.

"Did you take anything at tiffin?" said Lutyens, and the team shook their heads. They were too dry to talk.

"All right. The Archangels did. They are worse pumped than we are."

"They've got the better ponies," said Powell. "I shan't be sorry when this business is over."

That fifth quarter was a sad one in every way. Faiz Ullah played like a little red demon; and the Rabbit seemed to be everywhere at once, and Benami rode straight at anything and everything that came in his way, while the umpires on their ponies wheeled like gulls outside the shifting game. But the Archangels had the better mounts—they had kept their racers till late in the game—and never allowed the Skidars to play football. They hit the ball up and down the width of the ground till Benami and the rest were outpaced. Then they went forward, and time and again Lutyens and Grey Dawn were just, and only just, able to send the ball away with a long splitting back-hander. Grey Dawn forgot that he was an Arab; and turned from grey to blue as he galloped. Indeed, he forgot too well, for he did not keep his eyes on the ground as an Arab should, but stuck out his nose and scuttled for the dear honour of the game. They had watered the ground once or twice between the quarters, and a careless waterman had emptied the last of his skinfull all in one place near the Skidars' goal. It was close to the end of play, and for the tenth time Grey Dawn was bolting after a ball when his near hind foot slipped on the grassy mud and he rolled over and over, pitching Lutyens just clear of the goal-post; and the triumphant Archangels made their goal. Then time was called—two goals all; but Lutyens had to be helped up, and Grey Dawn rose with his near hind leg strained somewhere.

"What's the damage?" said Powell, his arm round Lutyens.

"Collar-bone, of course," said Lutyens between his teeth. It was the third time he had broken it in two years, and it hurt him.

Powell and the others whistled. "Game's up," said Hughes.

"Hold on. We've five good minutes yet, and it isn't my right hand," said Lutyens. "We'll stick it out."

"I say," said the captain of the Archangels, trotting up. "Are you hurt, Lutyens? We'll wait if you care to put in a substitute. I wish—I mean—the fact is, you fellows deserve this game if any team does. Wish we could give you a man or some of our ponies—or something."

"You're awfully good, but we'll play it to a finish, I think."

The captain of the Archangels stared for a little. "That's not half bad," he said, and went back to his own side, while Lutyens borrowed a scarf from one of his native officers and made a sling of it. Then an Archangel galloped up with a big bath-sponge and advised Lutyens to put it under his arm-pit to ease his shoulder, and between them they tied up his left arm scientifically, and one of the native officers leaped forward with four long glasses that fizzed and bubbled.

The team looked at Lutyens piteously, and he nodded. It was the last quarter, and nothing would matter after that. They drank out the dark golden drink, and wiped their moustaches, and things looked more hopeful.

The Maltese Cat had put his nose into the front of Lutyens' shirt and was trying to say how sorry he was.

"He knows," said Lutyens, proudly. "The beggar knows. I've played him without a bridle before now—for fun."

"It's no fun now," said Powell. "But we haven't a decent substitute."

"No," said Lutyens. "It's the last quarter, and we've got to make our goal and win. I'll trust the Cat."

"If you fall this time you'll suffer a little," said Macnamara.

"I'll trust the Cat," said Lutyens.

"You hear that?" said the Maltese Cat proudly to the others. "It's worth while playing polo for ten years to have that said of you. Now then, my sons, come along. We'll kick up a little bit, just to show the Archangels *this* team haven't suffered."

And, sure enough, as they went on to the ground the Maltese Cat, after satisfying himself that

Polo Players in India, 1891, R. Caton Woodville

Lutyens was home in the saddle, kicked out three or four times, and Lutyens laughed. The reins were caught up anyhow in the tips of his strapped hand, and he never pretended to rely on them. He knew the Cat would answer to the least pressure of the leg, and by way of showing off—for his shoulder hurt him very much—he bent the little fellow in a close figure-of-eight in and out between the goal-posts. There was a roar from the native officers and men, who dearly loved a piece of *dugabashi* (horse-trick work), as they called it, and the pipes very quietly and scornfully drowned out the first bars of a common bazaar-tune called "Freshly Fresh and Newly New", just as a warning to the other regiments that the Skidars were fit. All the natives laughed.

"And now," said the Cat as they took their place, "remember that this is the last quarter, and follow the ball."

"Don't need to be told," said Who's Who.

"Let me go on. All those people on all four sides will begin to crowd in—just as they did at Malta. You'll hear people calling out, and moving forward and being pushed back, and that is going to make the Archangel ponies very unhappy. But if a ball is struck to the boundary, you go after it and let the people get out of your way. I went over the pole of a four-in-hand once, and picked a game out of the dust by it. Back me up when I run, and follow the ball."

There was a sort of an all-round sound of sympathy and wonder as the last quarter opened, and then there began exactly what the Maltese Cat had foreseen. People crowded in close to the boundaries, and the Archangels' ponies kept looking sideways at the narrowing space. If you know how a man feels to be cramped at tennis—not because he wants to run out of the court, but because he likes to know that he can at a pinch—you will guess how ponies must feel when they are playing in a box of human beings.

"I'll bend some of those men if I can get away," said Who's Who, as he rocketed behind the ball; and Bamboo nodded without speaking. They were playing the last ounce in them, and the Maltese Cat had left the goal undefended to join them. Lutyens gave him every order that he could to bring him back, but this was the first time in his career that the little wise grey had ever played polo on his own responsibility, and he was going to make the most of it.

"What are you doing here?" said Hughes, as the Cat crossed in front of him and rode off an Archangel.

"The Cat's in charge—mind the goal!" shouted Lutyens, and bowing forward hit the ball full, and followed on, forcing the Archangels towards their own goal.

"No football," said the Cat. "Keep the ball by the boundaries and cramp 'em. Play open order and drive 'em to the boundaries."

Across and across the ground in big diagonals flew the ball, and whenever it came to a flying rush and a stroke close to the boundaries the Archangel ponies moved stiffly. They did not care to go headlong at a wall of men and carriages, though they could have turned on a sixpence.

"Wriggle her up the sides," said the Cat. "Keep her close to the crowd. They hate the carriages. Shikast, keep her up this side."

Shikast with Powell lay left and right behind the uneasy scuffle of an open scrimmage, and every time the ball was hit away Shikast galloped on it at such an angle that Powell was forced to hit it towards the boundary; and when the crowd had been driven away from that side, Lutyens would send the ball over the other, Shikast would slide desperately after it till his friends came down to help. It was billiards, and not football, this time—billiards in a corner pocket; and the cues were not well chalked.

"If they get us out in the middle of the ground they'll walk away from us. Dribble her along the sides," cried the Cat.

So they dribbled all along the boundary, where a pony could not come on their right-hand

A Game of Polo in India, 1895, John Charlton

side; and the Archangels were furious, and the umpires had to neglect the game to shout at the people to get back, and several blundering mounted policemen tried to restore order, all close to the scrimmage, and the nerves of the Archangels' ponies stretched and broke like cobwebs.

Five or six times an Archangel hit the ball up into the middle of the ground, and each time the watchful Shikast gave Powell his chance to send it back, and after each return, when the dust had settled, men could see that the Skidars had gained a few yards.

Every now and again there were shouts of "'Side! Off side!" from the spectators, but the teams were too busy to care, and the umpires had all they could do to keep their maddened ponies clear of the scuffle.

At last Lutyens missed a short easy stroke, and the Skidars had to fly back helter-skelter to protect their own goal, Shikast leading. Powell stopped the ball with a backhander when it was not fifty yards from the goal-posts, and Shikast spun round with a wrench that nearly hoisted Powell out of his saddle.

"Now's our last chance," said the Cat, wheeling like a cockchafer on a pin. "We've got to ride it out. Come along."

Lutyens felt the little chap take a deep breath, and, as it were, crouch under his rider. The ball was hopping towards the right-hand boundary, and an Archangel riding for it with both spurs and a whip, but neither spur nor whip would make his pony stretch himself as he neared the crowd. The Maltese Cat glided under his very nose, picking up his hind legs sharp, for there was not a foot to spare between his quarters and the other pony's bit. It was as neat an exhibition as fancy figure-skating. Lutyens hit with all the strength he had left, but the stick slipped a little in his hand, and the ball flew off to the left instead of keeping close to the boundary. Who's Who was far across the ground, thinking hard as he galloped. He repeated, stride for stride, the Cat's manœuvres with another Archangel pony, nipping the ball away from under his bridle, and clearing his opponent by half a fraction of an inch, for Who's Who was clumsy behind. Then he drove away towards the right as the Maltese Cat came up from the left; and Bamboo held a middle course exactly between them. The three were making a sort of Government-broad-arrow-shaped attack; and there was only the Archangels' back to guard the goal; but immediately behind them were three Archangels racing for all they knew, and mixed up with them was Powell, sending Shikast along on what he felt was their last hope. It takes a very good man to stand up to the rush of seven crazy ponies in the last quarter of a cup game, when men are riding with their necks for sale, and the ponies are delirious. The Archangels' back missed his stroke, and pulled aside just in time to let the rush go by. Bamboo and Who's Who shortened stride to give the Maltese Cat room, and Lutyens got the goal with a clean, smooth, smacking stroke that was heard all over the field. But there was no stopping the ponies. They poured through the goal-posts in one mixed mob, winners and losers together, for the pace had been terrific. The Maltese Cat knew by experience what would happen, and, to save Lutyens, turned to the right with one last effort that strained a back-sinew beyond hope of repair. As he did so he heard the right-hand goal-post crack as a pony cannoned into it—crack, splinter, and fall like a mast. It had been sawed three parts through in case of accidents, but it upset the pony nevertheless, and he blundered into another, who blundered into the left-hand post, and then there was confusion and dust and wood. Bamboo was lying on the ground, seeing stars; an Archangel pony rolled beside him, breathless and angry; Shikast had sat down dog-fashion to avoid falling over the others, and was sliding along on his little bobtail in a cloud of dust; and Powell was sitting on the ground, hammering with his stick and trying to cheer. All the others were shouting at the top of what was left of their voices, and the men who had been spilt were shouting too. As soon as the people saw no one was hurt, ten thousand native and English shouted and clapped and yelled, and before anyone could stop them the pipers of the Skidars broke on to the ground, with all the native officers and men behind them, and marched up and down, playing a wild northern tune called "Zakhme Bagān", and through the insolent blaring of the pipes and the high-pitched native yells you could hear the Archangels' band hammering, "For they are all jolly good fellows" and then reproachfully to the losing team "Ooh, Kafoozalum! Kafoozalum! Kafoozalum!"

Besides all these things and many more, there was a Commander-in-Chief, and an Inspector-General of Cavalry, and the principal veterinary officer in all India, standing on the top of a regimental coach, yelling like school-boys; and brigadiers and colonels and commissioners, and hundreds of pretty ladies joined the chorus. But the Maltese Cat stood with his head down, wondering how many legs were left to him; and Lutyens watched the men and ponies pick themselves out of the wreck of the two goal-posts, and he patted the Cat very tenderly.

"I say," said the captain of the Archangels, spitting a pebble out of his mouth, "will you take three thousand for that pony—as he stands?"

"No, thank you. I've an idea he's saved my life," said Lutyens, getting off and lying down at full length. Both teams were on the ground too, waving their boots in the air and coughing and drawing deep breaths, as the *saises* ran up to take away the ponies, and an officious water-carrier sprinkled the players with dirty water till they sat up.

"My Aunt!" said Powell, rubbing his back and looking at the stumps of the goal-posts, "that was a game!"

They played it over again, every stroke of it, that night at the big dinner, when the Free-for-All Cup was filled and passed down the table, and emptied and filled again, and everybody made most eloquent speeches. About two in the morning, when there might have been some singing, a wise little, plain little, grey little head looked in through the open door.

"Hurrah! Bring him in," said the Archangels; and his *sais*, who was very happy indeed, patted the Maltese Cat on the flank, and he limped in to the blaze of light and the glittering uniforms, looking for Lutyens. He was used to messes, and men's bedrooms, and places where ponies are not usually encouraged, and in his youth had jumped on and off a mess-table for a bet. So he behaved himself very politely, and ate bread dipped in salt, and was petted all round the table, moving gingerly; and they drank his health, because he had done more to win the Cup than any man or horse on the ground.

That was glory and honour enough for the rest of his days, and the Maltese Cat did not complain much when his veterinary surgeon said that he would be no good for polo any more. When Lutyens married, his wife did not allow him to play, so he was forced to umpire; and his pony on these occasions was a flea-bitten grey with a neat polo-tail, lame all round, but desperately quick on his feet, and, as everybody knew, Past Pluperfect Prestissimo Player of the Game.

Bengal Lancer

F. Yeats-Brown

At last the boar breaks again, taking us over the road-menders' pits, and across the canal: ahead lies a branch of the Ganges. The Devil slithers down a sand-bank and plunges with a snort of joy into the water. None of the others will face it: there's an ungentlemanly pleasure in that.

This boar is a very good swimmer. So is The Devil. I leave his head free, holding the cantle of the saddle and my spear in my right hand, and paddling with my legs and left arm. How delicious this cold water feels, through my clothes, down into my boots. With a squelch I am in saddle again, everything running and dripping. That's a stone handicap to our friend, but I'll catch him yet.

He's making for the *jhow* along the river-bank. Blind going, and I'm alone.

The Collector has crossed, but he's far behind. A long rein and easy seat—The Devil must stand up without my help. I can see nothing in this sea of *jhow* except the ridge of the boar's back. There's no skill in riding such a country: nothing avails but a good horse, and good luck.

I have no luck. Just as we clear the *jhow*, and I am gaining, green branches and white sand hit me in the face. The Devil has caught his foot in a twisted root, and fallen, but I have the reins. I'm out of the hunt. My fingers are a nasty yellow colour with the cold water. I wish I'd had some sleep and breakfast. The Collector is on the boar now, and another spear is riding wide, expecting a jink. The boar is winded. He'll charge. Yes, but the Collector's missed him.

I'll have one more ride on The Devil. Whoa, lad. That's better. I've soused down into the saddle, gathered the wet reins, and am off again. After this ride, it will be nine months before I feel the lift of his loins, and the snatch of his bridle as he judges the approach to a ditch. I need a rest. Indian earth is hard to fall on. I have swallowed much of it, too, and my loins ache. Am I growing old?

No, by God not yet! The boar's jinked again, away from the other spear and (oh, exultation incomparable!) towards me.

The Devil has the legs of the others, and of the boar. Steadily we draw nearer. There is no cover here, and the boar is blown.

We draw level. The boar's mouth is open—in another two lengths those big tusks of his will furrow the sand. He's charged. He's come up my spear. I can feel his breath on my hand. I've killed, I think, but why doesn't The Devil go on?

Why *doesn't* The Devil go on?

This riding, and fall, and riding again seems to have happened ages ago, but we are still on the same spot. The boar charged. I dropped my spear, didn't I? Still The Devil is anchored, going up and down like a hobby horse.

My poor Devil—why didn't I guess? When the boar turned over, a foot of spear entered your belly by the girth. Poor Devil.

Isn't that better now I'm off your back? You are not dying, my friend?

The Devil's forelegs were straddled and his proud head was sunk between them. He shook himself and lay down. He stretched himself out, as if he knew that the day's work was over. I staunched his wound with my handkerchief: immediately it became a sop of blood. He gave a little whinny, as if I had brought him corn.

Then his eyes glazed.

A stimulant might have saved him, if only Lashkman Piari with her medicine chest had been visible. The life was still there in him, but dammed up somehow in the sensitive nerves, so that the heart would not beat.

A Lion Hunt, E. J. H. Vernet

I waited by him, helpless. Kites circled above us. They knew. His life had gone out of my reach, leaving carrion where fleetness and fire had been an instant before. It was the suddenness of it that was horrible; the knowledge that the ripple of his muscles and the swish of his tail and the pride of his eyes and the sweep of his stride were still close to me, although separated from reality by the time-lag of a nervous reflex. I sat still, not smoking, not thinking, growing gradually stony-hearted. Twilight came, and at last the elephants.

We hoisted The Devil on to Lashkman Piari's pad. Flies followed us back to camp.

FROM

Broken Record

Roy Campbell

The only thing good that I had met in Paris was the fine Russian Cossacks who had been poor and very thirsty on my last visit: and I had shared my money with them. They were my only friends, they recognized me from about a mile off. I was very much of their disposition and liked singing and dancing.

It happened that the "American Cowboys" were in Paris at the same time as I came back to find my Russian friends. Foolishly, the American cowboys had made a challenge and I was the first man in Paris to undertake the challenge. I was speaking to the horse in English, which it could understand, because it was an American buckjumper, and I broke it down in five minutes, simply by slitting its jaws with an ordinary snaffle. Its mane had been black-leaded, as I could smell, and its whole skin had been operated on by a surgeon, so it was like a silk shirt or the skin of a calf without ligaments. I went to the manager and took 3,000 francs off him—2,000 for the prize and 1,000 never to ride again against his company. I said, "You are a silly ass launching challenges. Everybody comes to admire, not to be challenged."

I found out from one of their cowboys that they were going to Lyon. One of my Cossack friends, Denisoff, said, "Let's follow these cowboys to Lyon."

"No," I said, "I have 1,000 to keep away."

"Well, you needn't *ride*," he says; so I went.

At Lyon there were hundreds of Russians. I was in my element. One Cossack song and dance for one Scottish song and reel. We were fine: but when the cowboys came they did not launch their challenge again, so we launched it.

Denis and Simeon said, "the horses are tame."

The manager was furious. "Tame!" he shouted.

Bareback Riders, W. H. Brown

"Yes, tame," said Simeon, "in our country we call these horses tame."

"Where do you come from?"

"Russia."

I was hiding behind Simeon and had 2,000 francs left. "Bet him 1,000," I said. We had been bingeing the money—2,000 in two days and none of us were well. But I had constated the horse very well, and Denis had noticed that in bucking he hooked towards the right always, as if his left hind leg were stronger than his right. Also the matter of his loose skin. At the apex of his buck, one had a furious lurch to the left. His tactic was to increase the lurch before it could be righted and go on adding it up. Also his mane and tail were covered with black lead, for polishing stoves, so there was no gripping him. His name was "The Zebra Dun". I remembered too that his lips must be terribly tender still, as they were bleeding when I left him. And we had planned now that every time he bucked, one must yank furiously to split him between the jaws and trust to the pain stopping him. The manager was forced to take on the bet: and he did not suspect my complicity.

[111]

Denisoff began well: he staggered the horse, which was simple-minded and furious, not an intelligent horse. If Denis had been a simple rider like me, he might have beaten him. I had beaten brutality and strength by brutality and strength (and some kindness mixed in) without using any intelligence (which I had reserved), only using animal reflexes. The horse came perpendicular and tried to fall back and roll on Denis, but each time he got off and on. His saddle was now almost hanging under the horse's belly, but he had worked his left foot like a spade between the girth and the ribs: the end of the five minutes was now approaching and our 1,000 was well over the horizon, with more singing and dancing and drinking and strumming the guitar.

Suddenly, however, Denisoff took a rakish angle like a feather in a lady's hat. That lady began arguing a bit, nodding, and so on, and soon Denisoff was down. His foot had been terribly wrenched in the fall and we lost 1,000 francs. The manager was purple with triumph. "That will teach the bastards," he was yelling in English. The horse, grinning like a donkey, was rushing towards Denisoff, who was staggering to his feet. It gave him a fearful bite on the shoulders and boxed him with its two front feet so that I thought poor Denis was dead and my last money gone to bury him. Simeon was over the barricade fighting the horse: he had it by the saddle and the bridle. I fetched off Denis, but was not recognized (a rare thing with me) by the manager. Denis was sprained in the ankle, bashed in the buttock, bitten in the shoulder, rubbed in the face: half of his moustache had been scrubbed off on the floor—he was exactly like a walrus with only one tusk. Two lawyers in the audience rushed at Denis to tell him he could get damages etc. Until then I had not imagined how dirty lawyers could be, always thinking, even at a spectacle, about swindling, fining or damaging people—like crows on a battlefield.

Meanwhile, to deride us, the manager's little daughter was riding the "Zebra Dun" round the ring to the huge applause of the Lyonnais. The "Zebra" was grinning like a donkey. The manager was shouting and challenging again. So Simeon took him up, but not for a bet. The manager, carried away again, had said, "I will give 1,000 to anyone who can ride him."

Simeon came into the ring and the horse rushed at him to box him with his front hoofs. Simeon had to run away and everyone laughed. But Simeon fenced in and jumped, hooking the "Zebra" in a very correct manner with his legs. The "Zebra" started his tricks, but Simeon's legs were amazing—they seemed to be locked (like a dentist's forceps) on that horse. Leaning on the barrier, I swear I could see the third rank of the audience opposite under its belly. The horse did not have legs any more—it was a mixture of a porpoise and a boomerang. But if it had bucked Simeon off, its whole spine would have been extracted. Five minutes up, we got our money back. I was astounded at Simeon. I fancy myself as a rider, and especially as an equestrian acrobat—but until I saw Lescot and Saurel, and Don Simão de Veiga, I did not imagine it was possible to ride like that without punishing and bleeding the horse. The cowboys were good fellows; they did not care twopence, and disliked their manager: and they helped to drink our money. They were fine riders, no doubt, but inferior mentally to us South Africans, to the Mexicans, the Provençaux, and the South Americans who, among equestrian races, are the finest poets, and equestrian poetry is a completely different thing from that of the towns or the country in Europe.

FROM

The Beatrice Mystery

Derek Johns

It was six when the parade began. It was quite sudden and unexpected. A tremendous cheer was raised, and everyone turned to its source. I saw two men who dashed from a street leading onto the square and began to twirl enormous flags above their heads in complicated patterns. After a few moments the flags were hurled high into the air, thirty or forty feet, falling gracefully earthwards, stabilized by the weight of their staves, to be caught again by the ensigns.

"They are the *sbandieratori*," said Catherine. Her tone was conciliatory now. "Each *contrada* has two. We'll see them all."

The ensigns were preceded by a drummer, whom I hadn't at first seen, and followed by a mounted rider and a footman. They wore mediaeval costume in the colours of their flags.

The Race of the Palio (detail), Giovanni di Francesco Toscani

[113]

"Together they are called the *comparse*," said Catherine. "There's a captain, and several pages. The rider is mounted on a parade-horse. The racehorses are being kept in the mayor's courtyard."

The leading ensigns had progressed some way along the first side of the square, and into the space behind the *comparse* ran two more ensigns, dressed in different colours, who followed the same pattern of movements. Within twenty minutes the entire track was filled with these men. The height to which the flags were thrust could only fully be appreciated when the ensigns reached our corner of the square. The men wore long wigs under their caps, and looked immensely proud and haughty. Siena, the great city that had defeated the Florentines at the battle of Montaperti in 1260, Siena, the city that resisted heroically the forces of Charles V in 1554, lived again.

It was more than an hour before the seventeen *comparse* had taken their turn round the square. They were followed by the chariot drawn by four white oxen in which was carried the *palio* itself, the painted silk cloth that was the only prize. There was a lot of trumpeting, and a final flourish of the seventeen flags. As everyone dispersed, the racehorses appeared from the portal of the courtyard.

"They receive scourges as they come out, to incite them," said Catherine. "The rules state that on the first lap the riders are not allowed to whip their rivals' horses, attempt to unseat them, gouge out their eyes, or anything like that. After the first lap, anything goes."

She was standing on her toes so as to get a better view. The start was good, and they were away. One horse established a lead, and took the sharp turn by us about five yards ahead of the rest. By the time it came round again it was ten or more yards ahead. In the knot immediately behind there was a lot of shoving, and I saw whips lashing out in all directions. Suddenly one of the riders was unseated, and in an attempt to avoid him another rider also lost his reins and fell. A horse stumbled, and in a moment every horse and rider was down. The riders behind were able to get by, but their progress was slowed. The instant the last horse had passed, white-coated men with stretchers rushed onto the track, dragging off the riders before the leader came round for the last time. Three of the horses were up and running, but the others were still down on the track. The leader cut through them as though they weren't there, turning for the finish line. He was thirty yards or more ahead of the others now, and uncatchable. The cries that went up as he crossed the line were sporadic but joyful, and where they were heard I could see flags raised again, flags the colour of the rider's costume. The race had lasted less than a minute.

The Cowboy

Philip Ashton Rollins

Scattered about the West were "spoiled horses," animals which man, by kicks in the face or by other abuse during the breaking period, had ruined as to character, and which, engraving on their hearts the motto, "No one shall ever stay on our backs," held throughout their lives as closely as they could to their resolve and bucked and bucked and bucked. They were merely man-made "outlaws."

"Bucking" was synonymous with "pitching," there being no difference except that of geography. The Northwesterner called the horrid motion "bucking" or "buck jumping," the Texan termed it "pitching." "Casueying," as a further synonym, flourished a while in southern Texas, but rarely wandered beyond the region of its birth.

Pitching, if it consisted merely of violent motion, would need little description beyond that it was like the antics of an angry cat on a hot plate, or, in June Buzzell's words, was "a twin sister to delirium tremens on a circular staircase." Jack Tansy, having subdued a particularly turbulent beast, gaspingly announced from his saddle that he had been "settin' on three epileptic fits roarin' inside a single horsehide." Tex Whiting, on another occasion, averred that his own horse had "just nacherly druv my pants' seat clean through my hat crown," and it was reported that Jim Cowell "got throwed so far he didn't get back in time for his own funeral." There was indeed significance in the Western phrase, "Bucking off a porous plaster." A less fervid picturing lay in the Englishman's confession: "The beasty lowered 'is 'ead, 'umped 'is back, and Hi didn't remain."

The violence of bucking was measured not so much by the mere loftiness, length and speed of the horse's jumps, as it was by the abrupt side thrusts and sudden changes of direction and rhythm which imposed pitiless strains upon the abdomen of the rider and viciously twitched his neck.

As for the loftiness of the jumps, a pitching horse ordinarily did not at any one instant have all of itself at any great height in the air. During the moment that the beast's front hoofs were flung farthest upward, its relatively quiescent hind legs would be on or near the ground. An instant later, while the rear feet were pointed skyward, the front ones would be close to earth. When a pitching horse, entirely in the air, attained the posture of a drowned feline lifted by the middle of its back, and had all four legs hanging straight downward, all four hoofs on the same horizontal plane, if that plane were twenty-four inches above the ground, the spectators would applaud. And if it were thirty-six inches, local punchers would talk for years about that horse and it would gain admission to the honor roll of equine cussedness, would have West-wide reputation.

The Bronco Buster, Frederic Remington

Its name would be enshrined with those of Steamboat, Flying Devil, Undertaker's Pet, Leprosy, Gut Buster, Cholera Morbus, Appendicitis, Ulcerated Tooth, Gangrene, Annihilation, Sudden Death, Gentle Lizzie, all of sainted memory; with that of infamous Long Tom, with that of No Name, a prominent grave-digger of a more recent day.

Bucking could be made the more aggressive by eccentrically intermingling high jumps with low, long jumps with short, and by frequent erratic alterations in their speed and direction.

The most telling element in producing violence was, however, the ability of crafty horses to leap with definite uniform time-beat, coerce the rider's body into synchronization, and then abruptly alter the beat. If this instant variation in rhythm was coincident, as it commonly was, with a pronounced change in the direction and velocity of the leaps, the rider "needed glue on his pants." And, if there was the added element of either a vicious side thrust or a demoniac vibratory spasm along the bronco's backbone, there was much greater need for the glue. This trinary combination of discomforting actions was defined in musical terminology by Slim Brown, a tireless virtuoso on the mouth-organ at the bunk house. He styled it a "syncopated gizzard popper." Extremely proficient in this intricate method of saddle emptying was the late-lamented Rigor Mortis, a wall-eyed stallion which Montana Bill somewhat illogically described as "a high-falutin' primy donna in hellishness."

Thus it was that an iniquitous director of violence was the mental adroitness of the horse. If the beast was extremely ingenious, it could demand from its rider much more than mere courage, control of balance and unlimited physical endurance, for it had ability to sense its rider's innate tempo and foibles, and, plotting against them, to produce, at the exact moment least convenient for the rider, the motion which, at that instant, was most disconcerting to him. Such well-devised gyrations, known as "fancy steps," varied with the horses that invented them, and could not be taught by man. Under conditions of the sort we have mentioned, the contest became one of brains, the brains of the man pitted against those of the horse. Given a beast with all this acumen, agility and repertoire, and you have the classic, impish pitcher of the Western plains, the "bronc with a bagful of private tricks" and with knowledge when and where to open it; the self-educated, unscrupulous devil for which every old-time ranchman had pride, affection and a curse.

5

Horse Trading

I have known a party of Sioux to steal the horses of a buffalo-hunting outfit, whereupon the latter retaliated by stealing the horses of a party of harmless Grosventres; and I knew a party of Cheyennes, whose horses had been taken by white thieves, to, in revenge, assail a camp of perfectly orderly cowboys. Most of the ranchmen along the Little Missouri in 1884 were pretty good fellows, who would not wrong Indians, yet they tolerated for a long time the presence of men who did not scruple to boast that they stole horses from the latter, while our peaceful neighbours, the Grosventres, likewise permitted two notorious red-skinned horse thieves to use their reservation as a harbour of refuge and a starting point from which to make forays against the cattlemen.

from The Winning of the West *by Theodore Roosevelt*

Kelso Horse Show

Maurice Lindsay

Morning discovers it, sprawled in a loop the river
swings itself through the meadow on. Already
horse-boxes, floats and cars have runnelled the edge
of the field to a slush of muddy grass. A steady
straggle of people thickens the booths and the ring.
April neighs coldness. White clouds scud
last winter off the skies. The show-ground shakes
to life as buyers, catalogued with hunches, thud
incautious canters, swerved by the boundary hedge.
Ponies nudge stakes, or rub a child's hand,
soft as their noses. Shouldering knotted halters
the sellers wait their turn behind the stand
where the auctioneer patters, hoarse with loss or profit.
Hunters and hacks parade reluctant paces,
plodding a clomped-up circle. The bidding sways
among five hands, then swings between two faces—
a fighting man whom enemy winds have leathered
smooth as a saddle; and in from the lean hills
a Border farmer—both of them aware
their urge for satisfaction is the will's
ability to knock down for a song
whatever each has set his heart upon,
though couldn't care for less as soon as got.
Down goes the Colonel's arrogance; down, down,
before a folly richer than his own.
Hard on the hunter's hooves, a gelding bears
reflections of so many hopeful selves
that most must be unbridled small despairs.
But sold or bought, the time and the place are the horses;
the sweet smell of their sweat, the strung hay
they munch their breath on, the patient stable darkness
rippling their flanks, commotions the livelong day
till it breaks away from its minute-by-minute grazing,
from Countified calls and bawdy Irish curses;

an image riding its own reality
to a sense of recognition no one rehearses;
and for all the human dressage, the play of purses,
something out of the past in me rejoices.

Kilkenny Horse Fair, Sir Alfred Munnings

Some Experiences of an Irish R.M.

E. Œ. Somerville & Martin Ross

A giggling group of country girls elbowed their way past us out of the crowd of spectators, one of the number inciting her fellows to hurry on to the other field "until they'd see the lads galloping the horses" to which another responding that she'd "be skinned alive for the horses", the party sped on their way. We—i.e. my wife, Miss Knox, Bernard Shute, and myself—followed in their wake, a matter by no means as easy as it looked. Miss Shute had exhibited her wonted intelligence by remaining on the hilltop with the *Spectator*: she had not reached the happy point of possessing a mind ten years older than her age, and a face ten years younger, without also developing the gift of scenting boredom from afar. We squeezed past the noses and heels of fidgety horses, and circumnavigated their attendant groups of critics, while half-trained brutes in snaffles bolted to nowhere and back again, and whinnying foals ran to and fro in search of their mothers.

A moderate bank divided the upper from the lower fields, and as every feasible spot in it was commanded by a refusing horse, the choice of a place and moment for crossing it required judgement. I got Philippa across it in safety; Miss Knox, though as capable as any young woman in Ireland of getting over a bank, either on horseback or on her own legs, had to submit to the assistance of Mr Shute, and the laws of dynamics decreed that a force sufficient to raise a bow anchor should hoist her seven stone odd to the top of the bank with such speed that she landed half on her knees and half in the arms of her pioneer. A group of portentously quiet men stood near, their eyes on the ground, their hands in their pockets; they were all dressed so much alike that I did not at first notice that Flurry Knox was among them; when I did, I perceived that his eyes, instead of being on the ground, were surveying Mr Shute with that measure of disapproval that he habitually bestowed upon strange men.

"You're later than I thought you'd be," he said. "I have a horse half-bought for Mrs Yeates. It's that old mare of Bobby Bennett's; she makes a little noise, but she's a good mare, and you couldn't throw her down if you tried. Bobby wants thirty pounds for her, but I think you might get her for less. She's in the hotel stables, and you can see her when you go to lunch."

We moved on towards the rushy bank of the river, and Philippa and Sally Knox seated themselves on a low rock, looking, in their white frocks, as incongruous in that dingy preoccupied assemblage as the dreamy meadow-sweet and purple spires of loosestrife that thronged the river banks. Bernard Shute had been lost in the shifting maze of men and horses, who were, for the most part, galloping with the blind fury of charging bulls; but presently, among a party who seemed

Carriages at the Races, Edgar Degas

to be riding the finish of a race, we descried our friend, and a second or two later he hauled a brown mare to a standstill in front of us.

"The fellow's asking forty-five pounds for her," he said to Miss Sally; "she's a nailer to gallop. I don't think it's too much?"

"Her grandsire was the Mountain Hare," said the owner of the mare, hurrying up to continue her family history, "and he was the grandest horse in the four baronies. He was forty-two years of age when he died, and they waked him the same as ye'd wake a Christian. They had whisky and porther—and bread—and a piper in it."

"Thim Mountain Hare colts is no great things," interrupted Mr Shute's groom contemptuously. "I seen a colt once that was one of his stock, and if there was forty men and their wives, and they after him with sticks, he wouldn't lep a sod of turf."

"Lep, is it!" ejaculated the owner in a voice shrill with outrage. "You may lead that mare out through the counthry, and there isn't a fence in it that she wouldn't go up to it as indepindent as if she was going to her bed, and your honour's ladyship knows that dam well, Miss Knox."

"You want too much money for her, McCarthy," returned Miss Sally, with her little air of preternatural wisdom.

"God pardon you, Miss Knox! Sure a lady like you knows well that forty-five pounds is no money for that mare. Forty-five pounds!" He laughed. "It'd be as good for me to make her a present to the gentleman all out as take three farthings less for her! She's too grand entirely for a poor farmer like me, and if it wasn't for the long weak family I have, I wouldn't part with her under twice the money."

"Three fine lumps of daughters in America paying his rent for him," commented Flurry in the background. "That's the long weak family!"

Bernard dismounted and slapped the mare's ribs approvingly.

"I haven't had such a gallop since I was at Rio," he said. "What do you think of her, Miss Knox?" Then, without waiting for an answer, "I like her. I think I may as well give him the forty-five and have done with it!"

At these ingenuous words I saw a spasm of anguish cross the countenance of McCarthy, easily interpreted as the first pang of a life-long regret that he had not asked twice the money. Flurry Knox put up an eyebrow and winked at me; Mr Shute's groom turned away for very shame. Sally Knox laughed with the deplorable levity of nineteen.

Thus, with a brevity absolutely scandalous in the eyes of all beholders, the bargain was concluded.

Flurry strolled up to Philippa, observing an elaborate remoteness from Miss Sally and Mr Shute.

"I believe I'm selling a horse here myself today," he said; "would you like to have a look at him, Mrs Yeates?"

"Oh, are you selling, Knox?" struck in Bernard, to whose brain the glory of buying a horse had obviously mounted like new wine; "I want another, and I know yours are the right sort."

"Well, as you seem fond of galloping," said Flurry sardonically, "this one might suit you."

"You don't mean the Moonlighter?" said Miss Knox, looking fixedly at him.

"Supposing I did, have you anything to say against him?" replied Flurry.

Decidedly he was in a very bad temper. Miss Sally shrugged her shoulders, and gave a little shred of a laugh, but said no more.

In a comparatively secluded corner of the field we came upon Moonlighter, sidling and fussing, with flickering ears, his tail tightly tucked in and his strong back humped in a manner that boded little good. Even to my untutored eye, he appeared to be an uncommonly good-looking animal, a well-bred grey, with shoulders that raked back as far as the eye could wish, the true Irish jumping hindquarters, and a showy head and neck; it was obvious that nothing except Michael Hallahane's adroit chucks at his bridle kept him from displaying his jumping powers free of charge. Bernard stared at him in silence; not the pregnant and intimidating silence of the connoisseur, but the tongue-tied muteness of helpless ignorance. His eye for horses had most probably been formed on circus posters, and the advertisements of a well-known embrocation, and Moonlighter approximated in colour and conduct to these models.

"I can see he's a ripping fine horse," he said at length; "I think I should like to try him."

Miss Knox changed countenance perceptibly, and gave a perturbed glance at Flurry. Flurry remained impenetrably unamiable.

"I don't pretend to be a judge of horses," went on Mr Shute. "I dare say I needn't tell *you* that!" with a very engaging smile at Miss Sally; "but I like this one awfully."

As even Philippa said afterwards, she would not have given herself away like that over buying a reel of cotton.

"Are you quite sure that he's really the sort of horse you want?" said Miss Knox, with rather more colour in her face than usual; "he's only four years old, and he's hardly a finished hunter."

The object of her philanthropy looked rather puzzled. "What! can't he jump?" he said.

"Is it jump?" exclaimed Michael Hallahane, unable any longer to contain himself; "is it the horse that jumped five foot of a clothes line in Heffernan's yard, and not a one on his back but himself, and didn't leave so much as the thrack of his hoof on the quilt that was hanging on it!"

"That's about good enough," said Mr Shute, with his large friendly laugh; "what's your price, Knox? I must have the horse that jumped the quilt! I'd like to try him, if you don't mind. There are some jolly-looking banks over there."

"My price is a hundred sovereigns," said Flurry, "you can try him if you like."

"Oh, don't!" cried Sally impulsively; but Bernard's foot was already in the stirrup. "I call it disgraceful!" I heard her say in a low voice to her kinsman—"you know he can't ride."

The kinsman permitted himself a malign smile. "That's his lookout," he said.

Perhaps the unexpected docility with which Moonlighter allowed himself to be manœuvred through the crowd was due to Bernard's thirteen stone; at all events, his progress through a gate into the next field was unexceptionable. Bernard, however, had no idea of encouraging this tranquillity. He had come out to gallop, and without further ceremony he drove his heels into Moonlighter's side, and took the consequences in the shape of a very fine and able buck. How he remained within even visiting distance of the saddle it is impossible to explain; perhaps his early experience in the rigging stood him in good stead in the matter of hanging on by his hands; but, however preserved, he did remain, and went away down the field at what he himself subsequently described as "the rate of knots".

Caledonian Cup, James Howe

Flurry flung away his cigarette and ran to a point of better observation. We all ran, including Michael Hallahane and various onlookers, and were in time to see Mr Shute charging the least advantageous spot in a hollow-faced furzy bank. Nothing but the grey horse's extreme activity got the pair safely over; he jumped it on a slant, changed feet in the heart of a furze-bush, and was lost to view. In what relative positions Bernard and his steed alighted was to us a matter of conjecture; when we caught sight of them again, Moonlighter was running away, with his rider still on his back, while the slope of the ground lent wings to his flight.

"That young gentleman will be apt to be killed," said Michael Hallahane with composure, not to say enjoyment.

"He'll be into the long bog with him pretty soon," said Flurry, his keen eye tracking the fugitive.

"Oh!—I thought he was off that time!" exclaimed Miss Sally, with a gasp in which consternation and amusement were blended. "There! He *is* into the bog!"

It did not take us long to arrive at the scene of disaster, to which, as to a dog-fight, other foot-runners were already hurrying, and on our arrival we found things looking remarkably unpleasant for Mr Shute and Moonlighter. The latter was sunk to his withers in the sheet of black slime into which he had stampeded; the former, submerged to the waist three yards further away in the bog, was trying to drag himself towards firm ground by the aid of tussocks of wiry grass.

"Hit him!" shouted Flurry. "Hit him! he'll sink if he stops there!"

Mr Shute turned on his adviser a face streaming with black mud, out of which his brown eyes and white teeth gleamed with undaunted cheerfulness.

"All jolly fine," he called back; "if I let go this grass I'll sink too!"

A shout of laughter from the male portion of the spectators sympathetically greeted this announcement, and a dozen equally futile methods of escape were suggested. Among those who had joined us was, fortunately, one of the many boys who pervaded the fair selling halters, and, by means of several of these knotted together, a line of communication was established. Moonlighter, who had fallen into the state of inane stupor in which horses in his plight so often indulge, was roused to activity by showers of stones and imprecations but faintly chastened by the presence of ladies. Bernard, hanging on to his tail, belaboured him with a cane, and, finally, the reins proving good, the task of towing the victims ashore was achieved.

"He's mine, Knox, you know," were Mr Shute's first words as he scrambled to his feet, "he's the best horse I ever got across—worth twice the money!"

"Faith, he's aisy plased!" remarked a bystander.

"Oh, do go and borrow some dry clothes," interposed Philippa practically; "surely there must be someone—"

"There's a shop in the town where he can strip a peg for 13s. 9d.," said Flurry grimly; "I wouldn't care myself about the clothes you'd borrow here!"

The morning sun shone jovially upon Moonlighter and his rider, caking momently the black bog stuff with which both were coated, and as the group disintegrated, and we turned to go back, every man present was pleasurably aware that the buttons of Mr Shute's riding breeches had burst at the knee, causing a large triangular hiatus above his gaiter.

"Well," said Flurry conclusively to me as we retraced our steps, "I always thought the fellow was a fool, but I never thought he was such a damned fool."

The Bible in Spain

George Borrow

We put up at a mean posada in the suburb for the purpose of refreshing our horses. Several cavalry soldiers were quartered there, who instantly came forth, and began, with the eyes of connoisseurs, to inspect my Andalusian entero. "A capital horse that would be for our troop," said the corporal; "what a chest he has! By what right do you travel with that horse, señor, when so many are wanted for the queen's service? He belongs to the requiso." "I travel with him by right of purchase, and being an Englishman," I replied. "Oh, your worship is an Englishman," answered the corporal; "that indeed alters the matter. The English in Spain are allowed to do what they please with their own, which is more than the Spaniards are. Cavalier, I have seen your countrymen in the Basque provinces. Vaya, what riders! what horses! They do not fight badly either. But their chief skill is in riding: I have seen them dash over barrancos to get at the factious, who thought themselves quite secure, and then they would fall upon them on a sudden and kill them to a man. In truth, your worship, this is a fine horse; I must look at his teeth."

I looked at the corporal—his nose and eyes were in the horse's mouth; the rest of the party, who might amount to six or seven, were not less busily engaged. One was examining his fore feet, another his hind; one fellow was pulling at his tail with all his might, while another pinched the windpipe, for the purpose of discovering whether the animal was at all touched there. At last, perceiving that the corporal was about to remove the saddle that he might examine the back of the animal, I exclaimed,—

"Stay, ye chabés of Egypt; ye forget that ye are hundunares, and are no longer paruguing grastes in the chardy."

The corporal at these words turned his face full upon me, and so did all the rest. Yes, sure enough, there were the countenances of Egypt, and the fixed, filmy stare of eye. We continued looking at each other for a minute at least, when the corporal, a villainous-looking fellow, at last said, in the richest gipsy whine imaginable, "The erray knows us, the poor Caloré! And he an Englishman! Bullati! I should not have thought that there was e'er a Busno would know us in these parts, where Gitános are never seen. Yes, your worship is right: we are all here of the blood of the Caloré. We are from Melegrana (Granada), your worship; they took us from thence and sent us to the wars. Your worship is right: the sight of that horse made us believe we were at home again in the mercado of Granada; he is a countryman of ours, a real Andalou. Por dios, your worship, sell us that horse; we are poor Caloré, but we can buy him."

"You forget that you are soldiers," said I. "How should you buy my horse?"

"We are soldiers, your worship," said the corporal, "but we are still Caloré; we buy and sell bestis; the captain of our troop is in league with us. We have been to the wars, but not to fight;

we left that to the Busné. We have kept together, and like true Caloré have stood back to back. We have made money in the wars, your worship. *No tenga usted cuidao* (Be under no apprehension). We can buy your horse."

Here he pulled out a purse, which contained at least ten ounces of gold.

"If I were willing to sell," I replied, "what would you give me for that horse?"

"Then your worship wishes to sell your horse? That alters the matter. We will give ten dollars for your worship's horse. He is good for nothing."

"How is this?" said I. "You this moment told me he was a fine horse—an Andalusian, and a countryman of yours."

"No, señor; we did not say that he was an Andalou. We said he was an Estremou, and the worst of his kind. He is eighteen years old, your worship, short-winded, and galled."

"I do not wish to sell my horse," said I. "Quite the contrary; I had rather buy than sell."

"Your worship does not wish to sell his horse," said the gipsy. "Stay, your worship; we will give sixty dollars for your worship's horse."

"I would not sell him for two hundred and sixty. Meclis! Meclis! say no more. I know your gipsy tricks. I will have no dealings with you."

The Horsemen, Honoré Daumier

"Did I not hear your worship say that you wished to buy a horse?" said the gipsy.

"I do not want to buy a horse," said I; "if I need anything, it is a pony to carry our baggage. But it is getting late.—Antonio, pay the reckoning."

"Stay, your worship; do not be in a hurry," said the gipsy. "I have got the very pony which will suit you."

Without waiting for my answer, he hurried into the stable, from whence he presently returned, leading an animal by a halter. It was a pony of about thirteen hands high, of a dark-red colour; it was very much galled all over, the marks of ropes and thongs being visible on its hide. The figure, however, was good, and there was an extraordinary brightness in its eye.

"There, your worship," said the gipsy—"there is the best pony in all Spain."

"What do you mean by showing me this wretched creature?" said I.

"This wretched creature," said the gipsy, "is a better horse than your Andalou!"

"Perhaps you would not exchange," said I, smiling.

"Señor, what I say is that he shall run with your Andalou, and beat him!"

"He looks feeble," said I; "his work is well-nigh done."

"Feeble as he is, señor, you could not manage him—no, nor any Englishman in Spain."

I looked at the creature again, and was still more struck with its figure. I was in need of a pony to relieve occasionally the horse of Antonio in carrying the baggage which we had brought from Madrid, and though the condition of this was wretched, I thought that by kind treatment I might possibly soon bring him round.

"May I mount this animal?" I demanded.

"He is a baggage-pony, señor, and is ill to mount. He will suffer none but myself to mount him, who am his master. When he once commences running, nothing will stop him but the sea. He springs over hills and mountains, and leaves them behind in a moment. If you will mount him, señor, suffer me to fetch a bridle, for you can never hold him in with a halter."

"This is nonsense," said I. "You pretend that he is spirited in order to enhance the price. I tell you his work is done."

I took the halter in my hand and mounted. I was no sooner on his back than the creature, who had before stood stone still, without displaying the slightest inclination to move, and who in fact gave no further indication of existence than occasionally rolling his eyes and pricking up an ear, sprang forward like a racehorse, at a most desperate gallop. I had expected that he might kick or fling himself down on the ground in order to get rid of his burden, but for this escapade I was quite unprepared. I had no difficulty, however, in keeping on his back, having been accustomed from my childhood to ride without a saddle. To stop him, however, baffled all my endeavours, and I almost began to pay credit to the words of the gipsy, who had said that he would run on until he reached the sea. I had, however, a strong arm, and I tugged at the halter until I compelled him to turn slightly his neck, which from its stiffness might almost have been of wood; he, however, did not abate his speed for a moment. On the left side of the road down which he dashed was a deep trench, just where the road took a turn towards the right, and over this he sprang in a sideward direction. The halter broke with the effort, the pony shot forward like an arrow, whilst I fell back into the dust.

"Señor," said the gipsy, coming up with the most serious countenance in the world, "I told you not to mount that animal unless well bridled and bitted. He is a baggage-pony, and will suffer none to mount his back, with the exception of myself who feed him." (Here he whistled, and the animal, who was skirring over the field and occasionally kicking up his heels, instantly returned with a gentle neigh.) "Now, your worship, see how gentle he is. He is a capital baggage-pony, and will carry all you have over the hills of Galicia."

"What do you ask for him?" said I.

"Señor, as your worship is an Englishman and a good ginete, and, moreover, understands the ways of the Caloré, and their tricks and their language also, I will sell him to you a bargain. I will take two hundred and sixty dollars for him, and no less."

"That is a large sum," said I.

"No, señor, not at all, considering that he is a baggage-pony, and belongs to the troop, and is not mine to sell."

FROM

The Virginian

Owen Wister

Balaam accompanied his guest, Shorty, when he went to the pasture to saddle up and depart. "Got a rope?" he asked the guest, as they lifted down the bars.

"Don't need to rope him. I can walk right up to Pedro. You stay back."

Hiding his bridle behind him, Shorty walked to the river-bank, where the pony was switching his long tail in the shade; and speaking persuasively to him, he came nearer, till he laid his hand on Pedro's dusky mane, which was many shades darker than his hide. He turned expectantly, and his master came up to his expectations with a piece of bread.

"Eats that, does he?" said Balaam, over the bars.

"Likes the salt," said Shorty. "Now, n-n-ow, here! Yu' don't guess yu'll be bridled, don't you? Open your teeth! Yu'd like to play yu' was nobody's horse and live private? Or maybe yu'd prefer ownin' a saloon?"

Pedro evidently enjoyed this talk, and the dodging he made about the bit. Once fairly in his mouth, he accepted the inevitable, and followed Shorty to the bars. Then Shorty turned and extended his hand.

"Shake!" he said to his pony, who lifted his forefoot quietly and put it in his master's hand. Then the master tickled his nose, and he wrinkled it and flattened his ears, pretending to bite. His face wore an expression of knowing relish over this performance. "Now the other hoof," said Shorty; and the horse and master shook hands with their left. "I learned him that," said the cowboy, with pride and affection. "Say, Pede," he continued, in Pedro's ear, "ain't yu' the best little horse in the country? What? Here, now! Keep out of that, you dead-beat! There ain't no more bread." He pinched the pony's nose, one-quarter of which was wedged into his pocket.

The Cowboy, Frederic Remington

"Quite a lady's little pet!" said Balaam, with the rasp in his voice. "Pity this isn't New York, now, where there's a big market for harmless horses. Gee-gees, the children call them."

"He ain't no gee-gee," said Shorty, offended. "He'll beat any cow-pony workin' you've got. Yu' can turn him on a half-dollar. Don't need to touch the reins. Hang 'em on one finger and swing your body, and he'll turn."

Balaam knew this, and he knew that the pony was only a four-year-old. "Well," he said, "Drybone's had no circus this season. Maybe they'd buy tickets to see Pedro. He's good for that, anyway."

Shorty became gloomy. The Virginian was grimly smoking. Here was something else going on not to his taste, but none of his business.

"Try a circus," persisted Balaam. "Alter your plans for spending cash in town, and make a little money instead."

Shorty, having no plans to alter and no cash to spend, grew still more gloomy.

"What'll you take for that pony?" said Balaam.

Shorty spoke up instantly. "A hundred dollars couldn't buy that piece of stale mud off his back," he asserted, looking off into the sky grandiosely.

But Balaam looked at Shorty. "You keep the mud," he said, "and I'll give you thirty dollars for the horse."

Shorty did a little professional laughing, and began to walk toward his saddle.

"Give you thirty dollars," repeated Balaam, picking a stone up and slinging it into the river.

"How far do yu' call it to Drybone?" Shorty remarked, stooping to investigate the bucking-strap on his saddle—a superfluous performance, for Pedro never bucked.

"You won't have to walk," said Balaam. "Stay all night, and I'll send you over comfortably in the morning, when the wagon goes for the mail."

"Walk!" Shorty retorted. "Drybone's twenty-five miles. Pedro'll put me there in three hours and not know he done it." He lifted the saddle on the horse's back. "Come, Pedro," said he.

"Come, Pedro!" mocked Balaam.

There followed a little silence.

"No, sir," mumbled Shorty, with his head under Pedro's belly, busily cinching. "A hundred dollars is bottom figures."

Balaam, in his turn, now duly performed some professional laughing, which was noted by Shorty under the horse's belly. He stood up and squared round on Balaam.

"Well, then," he said, "what'll yu' give for him?"

"Thirty dollars," said Balaam, looking far off into the sky, as Shorty had looked.

"Oh, come, now," expostulated Shorty.

It was he who now did the feeling for an offer, and this was what Balaam liked to see. "Why, yes," he said, "thirty," and looked surprised that he should have to mention the sum so often.

"I thought yu'd quit them first figures," said the cowpuncher, "for yu' can see I ain't goin' to look at 'em."

Balaam climbed on the fence and sat there. "I'm not crying for your Pedro," he observed dispassionately. "Only it struck me you were dead broke, and wanted to raise cash and keep yourself going till you hunted up a job and could buy him back." He hooked his right thumb inside his waistcoat pocket. "But I'm not cryin' for him," he repeated. "He'd stay right here, of course. I wouldn't part with him. Why does he stand that way? Hello!" Balaam suddenly straightened himself, like a man who has made a discovery.

"Hello, what?" said Shorty, on the defensive.

Balaam was staring at Pedro with a judicial frown. Then he stuck out a finger at the horse,

[133]

keeping the thumb hooked in his pocket. So meagre a gesture was felt by the ruffled Shorty to be no just way to point to Pedro. "What's the matter with that foreleg there?" said Balaam.

"Which? Nothin's the matter with it!" snapped Shorty.

Balaam climbed down from his fence and came over with elaborate deliberation. He passed his hand up and down the off foreleg. Then he spit slenderly. "Mm!" he said thoughtfully; and added, with a shade of sadness, "that's always to be expected when they're worked too young."

Shorty slid his hand slowly over the disputed leg. "What's to be expected?" he inquired— "that they'll eat hearty? Well, he does."

At this retort the Virginian permitted himself to laugh in audible sympathy.

"Sprung," continued Balaam, with a sigh. "Whirling round short when his bones were soft did that. Yes."

"Sprung!" Shorty said, with a bark of indignation. "Come on, Pede; you and me'll spring for town."

He caught the horn of the saddle, and as he swung into place the horse rushed away with him. "O-ee! yoi-yup, yup, yup!" sang Shorty, in the shrill cow dialect. He made Pedro play an exhibition game of speed, bringing him round close to Balaam in a wide circle, and then he vanished in dust down the left-bank trail.

Balaam looked after him and laughed harshly. He had seen trout dash about like that when the hook in their jaw first surprised them. He knew Shorty would show the pony off, and he knew Shorty's love for Pedro was not equal to his need of money. He called to one of his men, asked something about the dam at the mouth of the cañon, where the main irrigation ditch began, made a remark about the prolonged drought, and then walked to his dining-room door, where, as he expected, Shorty met him.

"Say," said the youth, "do you consider that's any way to talk about a good horse?"

"Any dude could see the leg's sprung," said Balaam. But he looked at Pedro's shoulder, which was well laid back; and he admired his points, dark in contrast with the buckskin, and also the width between the eyes.

"Now you know," whined Shorty, "that it ain't sprung any more than your leg's cork. If you mean the right leg ain't plumb straight, I can tell you he was born so. That don't make no difference, for it ain't weak. Try him onced. Just as sound and strong as iron. Never stumbles. And he don't never go to jumpin' with yu'. He's kind and he's smart." And the master petted his pony, who lifted a hoof for another handshake.

Of course Balaam had never thought the leg was sprung, and he now took on an unprejudiced air of wanting to believe Shorty's statements if he only could.

"Maybe there's two years' work left in that leg," he now observed.

"Better give your hawss away, Shorty," said the Virginian.

"Is this your deal, my friend?" inquired Balaam. And he slanted his bullet head at the Virginian.

"Give him away, Shorty," drawled the Southerner. "His laig is busted. Mr Balaam says so."

Balaam's face grew evil with baffled fury. But the Virginian was gravely considering Pedro. He, too, was not pleased. But he could not interfere. Already he had overstepped the code in these matters. He would have dearly liked—for reasons good and bad, spite and mercy mingled—to have spoiled Balaam's market, to have offered a reasonable or even an unreasonable price for Pedro, and taken possession of the horse himself. But this might not be. In bets, in card games, in all horse transactions and other matters of similar business, a man must take care of himself, and wiser onlookers must suppress their wisdom and hold their peace.

That evening Shorty again had a cigar. He had parted with Pedro for forty dollars, a striped

[134]

Horsemen on the Beach, Paul Gauguin

The Horse Fair, Rosa Bonheur and Nathalie Micas

The Trapper's Last Shot, William Ranney

Mexican blanket, and a pair of spurs. Undressing over in the bunk house, he said to the Virginian, "I'll sure buy Pedro back off him just as soon as ever I rustle some cash." The Virginian grunted. He was thinking he should have to travel hard to get the horses to the Judge by the 30th, and below that thought lay his aching disappointment and his longing for Bear Creek.

In the early dawn Shorty sat up among his blankets on the floor of the bunk house and saw the various sleepers coiled or sprawled in their beds; their breathing had not yet grown restless at the nearing of day. He stepped to the door carefully and saw the crowding blackbirds begin their walk and chatter in the mud of the littered and trodden corrals. From beyond among the cotton woods, came continually the smooth unemphatic sound of the doves answering each other invisibly; and against the empty ridge of the river-bluff lay the moon, no longer shining, for there was established a new light through the sky. Pedro stood in the pasture close to the bars. The cowboy slowly closed the door behind him, and sitting down on the step, drew his money out and idly handled it, taking no comfort just then from its possession. Then he put it back, and after dragging on his boots, crossed to the pasture, and held a last talk with his pony, brushing the cakes of mud from his hide where he had rolled, and passing a lingering hand over his mane. As the sounds of the morning came increasingly from tree and plain, Shorty glanced back to see that no one was yet out of the cabin, and then put his arms round the horse's neck, laying his head against him. For a moment the cowboy's insignificant face was exalted by the emotion he would never have let others see. He hugged tight this animal who was dearer to his heart than anybody in the world.

[135]

"Good-by, Pedro," he said—"good-by." Pedro looked for bread.

"No," said his master, sorrowfully, "not any more. Yu' know well I'd give it yu' if I had it. You and me didn't figure on this, did we, Pedro? Good-by!"

He hugged his pony again, and got as far as the bars of the pasture, but returned once more. "Good-by, my little horse, my dear horse, my little, little Pedro," he said, as his tears wet the pony's neck. Then he wiped them with his hand, and got himself back to the bunk house. After breakfast he and his belongings departed to Drybone, and Pedro from his field calmly watched this departure; for horses must recognize even less than men the black corners that their destinies turn. The pony stopped feeding to look at the mail-wagon pass by; but the master sitting in the wagon forebore to turn his head.

6

Horse Laughing

I know two things about the horse,
And one of them is rather coarse.

Anonymous

There was an Old Man of Nepaul
From his horse had a terrible fall;
But, though split quite in two,
With some very strong glue
They mended that Man of Nepaul.

Edward Lear

FROM

Further Fables for Our Time *and* The Thurber Carnival

James Thurber

A farm horse named Charles was led to town one day by his owner, to be shod. He would have been shod and brought back home without incident if it hadn't been for Eva, a duck, who was always hanging about the kitchen door of the farmhouse, eavesdropping, and never got anything quite right. Her farm-mates said of her that she had two mouths but only one ear.

On the day that Charles was led away to the smithy, Eva went quacking about the farm, excitedly telling the other animals that Charles had been taken to town to be shot.

"They're executing an innocent horse!" cried Eva. "He's a hero! He's a martyr! He died to make us free!"

"He was the greatest horse in the world," sobbed a sentimental hen.

"He just seemed like old Charley to me," said a realistic cow. "Let's not get into a moony mood."

"He was wonderful!" cried a gullible goose.

"What did he ever do?" asked a goat.

Eva, who was as inventive as she was inaccurate, turned on her lively imagination. "It was the butchers who led him off to be shot!" she shrieked. "They would have cut our throats while we slept if it hadn't been for Charles!"

"I didn't see any butchers, and I can see a burnt-out firefly on a moonless night," said a barn owl. "I didn't hear any butchers and I can hear a mouse walk across the moss."

"We must build a memorial to Charles the Great, who saved our lives," quacked Eva. And all the birds and beasts in the barnyard except the wise owl, the skeptical goat, and the realistic cow set about building a memorial.

Just then the farmer appeared in the lane, leading Charles, whose new shoes glinted in the sunlight.

It was lucky that Charles was not alone, for the memorial-builders might have set upon him with clubs and stones for replacing their hero with just plain old Charley. It was lucky, too, that they could not reach the barn owl, who quickly perched upon the weathervane of the barn, for none is so exasperating as he who is right. The sentimental hen and the gullible goose were the ones who finally called attention to the true culprit—Eva, the one-eared duck with two mouths.

[140]

Farm Animals, Adriaen van de Velde

The others set upon her and tarred and unfeathered her, for none is more unpopular than the bearer of sad tidings that turn out to be false.

Moral: Get it right or let it alone. The conclusion you jump to may be your own.

*   *   *   *   *

Q.   How would you feel if every time you looked up from your work or anything, there was a horse peering at you from behind something? He prowls about the house at all hours of the day and night. Doesn't seem worried about anything, merely wakeful. What should I do to discourage him?

Mrs Grace Voynton

A.   The horse is probably sad. Changing the flower decorations of your home to something less like open meadows might discourage him, but then I doubt whether it is a good idea to discourage a sad horse. In any case speak to him quietly when he turns up from behind things. Leaping at a horse in a house and crying "Roogi, roogi!" or "Whoosh!" would only result in breakage and bedlam. Of course you might finally get used to having him around, if the house is big enough for both of you.

*   *   *   *   *

Q. My husband paid a hundred and seventy-five dollars for this moose to a man in Dorset, Ontario, who said he had trapped it in the woods. Something is wrong with his antlers, for we have to keep twisting them back into place all the time. They're loose.   Mrs Oliphant Beatty
A. You people are living in a fool's paradise. The animal is obviously a horse with a span of antlers strapped on to his head. If you really want a moose, dispose of the horse; if you want to keep the horse, take the antlers off. Their constant pressure on his ears isn't a good idea.

Horse, silver pepperpot

Samuel Foote

A white horse and a beautiful woman are two troublesome things to manage: as the first is difficult to be kept clean: and the second, honest.

THE LONG TAILED STALLION
of Augustus II. King of Poland.

The Mane 9. and the Tail 12 Ells in length.

Frederick the Great of Prussia

A German singer! I should as soon expect to get pleasure from the neighing of my horse.

Horse Scratching Its Ear with Monkey on Its Back, 17th century Chinese

The Brogue

Saki

The hunting season had come to an end, and the Mullets had not succeeded in selling the Brogue. There had been a kind of tradition in the family for the past three or four years, a sort of fatalistic hope, that the Brogue would find a purchaser before the hunting was over; but seasons came and went without anything happening to justify such ill-founded optimism. The animal had been named Berserker in the earlier stages of its career; it had been rechristened the Brogue later on, in recognition of the fact that, once acquired, it was extremely difficult to get rid of. The unkinder wits of the neighbourhood had been known to suggest that the first letter of its name was superfluous. The Brogue had been variously described in sale catalogues as a light-weight hunter, a lady's hack, and, more simply, but still with a touch of imagination, as a useful brown gelding, standing 15.1. Toby Mullet had ridden him for four seasons with the West Wessex; you can ride almost any sort of horse with the West Wessex as long as it is an animal that knows the country. The Brogue knew the country intimately, having personally created most of the gaps that were to be met with in banks and hedges for many miles round. His manners and characteristics were not ideal in the hunting field, but he was probably rather safer to ride to hounds than he was as a hack on country roads. According to the Mullet family, he was not really road-shy, but there were one or two objects of dislike that brought on sudden attacks of what Toby called swerving sickness. Motors and cycles he treated with tolerant disregard, but pigs, wheelbarrows, piles of stones by the roadside, perambulators in a village street, gates painted too aggressively white, and sometimes, but not always, the newer kind of beehives, turned him aside from his tracks in vivid imitation of the zigzag course of forked lightning. If a pheasant rose noisily from the other side of a hedgerow the Brogue would spring into the air at the same moment, but this may have been due to a desire to be companionable. The Mullet family contradicted the widely prevalent report that the horse was a confirmed crib-biter.

It was about the third week in May that Mrs Mullet, relict of the late Sylvester Mullet, and mother of Toby and a bunch of daughters, assailed Clovis Sangrail on the outskirts of the village with a breathless catalogue of local happenings.

"You know our new neighbour, Mr Penricarde?" she vociferated; "awfully rich, owns tin mines in Cornwall, middle-aged and rather quiet. He's taken the Red House on a long lease and spent a lot of money on alterations and improvements. Well, Toby's sold him the Brogue!"

Clovis spent a moment or two in assimilating the astonishing news; then he broke out into unstinted congratulation. If he had belonged to a more emotional race he would probably have kissed Mrs Mullet.

"How wonderful lucky to have pulled it off at last! Now you can buy a decent animal. I've always said that Toby was clever. Ever so many congratulations."

"Don't congratulate me. It's the most unfortunate thing that could have happened!" said Mrs Mullet dramatically.

Clovis stared at her in amazement.

"Mr Penricarde," said Mrs Mullet, sinking her voice to what she imagined to be an impressive whisper, though it rather resembled a hoarse, excited squeak, "Mr Penricarde has just begun to pay attentions to Jessie. Slight at first, but now unmistakable. I was a fool not to have seen it sooner. Yesterday, at the Rectory garden party, he asked her what her favourite flowers were, and she told him carnations, and today a whole stack of carnations has arrived, clove and malmaison and lovely dark red ones, regular exhibition blooms, and a box of chocolates that he must have got on purpose from London. And he's asked her to go round the links with him tomorrow. And now, just at this critical moment, Toby has sold him that animal. It's a calamity!"

"But you've been trying to get the horse off your hands for years," said Clovis.

"I've got a houseful of daughters," said Mrs Mullet, "and I've been trying—well, not to get them off my hands, of course, but a husband or two wouldn't be amiss among the lot of them; there are six of them, you know."

"I don't know," said Clovis, "I've never counted, but I expect you're right as to the number; mothers generally know these things."

"And now," continued Mrs Mullet, in her tragic whisper, "when there's a rich husband-in-prospect imminent on the horizon Toby goes and sells him that miserable animal. It will probably kill him if he tries to ride it; anyway, it will kill any affection he might have felt towards any member of our family. What is to be done? We can't very well ask to have the horse back; you see, we praised it up like anything when we thought there was a chance of his buying it, and

[145]

The New Ride, J. E. Millais

said it was just the animal to suit him."

"Couldn't you steal it out of his stable and send it to grass at some farm miles away?" suggested Clovis. "Write 'Votes for Women' on the stable door, and the thing would pass for a Suffragette outrage. No one who knew the horse could possibly suspect you of wanting to get it back again."

"Every newspaper in the country would ring with the affair," said Mrs Mullet; "can't you imagine the headline, 'Valuable Hunter Stolen by Suffragettes'? The police would scour the countryside till they found the animal."

"Well, Jessie must try and get it back from Penricarde on the plea that it's an old favourite. She can say it was only sold because the stable had to be pulled down under the terms of an old repairing lease, and that now it has been arranged that the stable is to stand for a couple of years longer."

"It sounds a queer proceeding to ask for a horse back when you've just sold him," said Mrs Mullet, "but something must be done, and done at once. The man is not used to horses, and I believe I told him it was as quiet as a lamb. After all, lambs go kicking and twisting about as if they were demented, don't they?"

"The lamb has an entirely unmerited character for sedateness," agreed Clovis.

Jessie came back from the golf links next day in a state of mingled elation and concern.

"It's all right about the proposal," she announced, "he came out with it at the sixth hole. I said I must have time to think it over. I accepted him at the seventh."

"My dear," said her mother, "I think a little more maidenly reserve and hesitation would have been advisable, as you've known him so short a time. You might have waited till the ninth hole."

"The seventh is a very long hole," said Jessie; "besides, the tension was putting us both off our game. By the time we'd got to the ninth hole we'd settled lots of things. The honeymoon is to be spent in Corsica, with perhaps a flying visit to Naples if we feel like it, and a week in London to wind up with. Two of his nieces are to be asked to be bridesmaids, so with our lot there will be seven, which is rather a lucky number. You are to wear your pearl grey, with any amount of Honiton lace jabbed into it. By the way, he's coming over this evening to ask your consent to the whole affair. So far all's well, but about the Brogue it's a different matter. I told him the legend about the stable, and how keen we were about buying the horse back, but he seems equally keen

Mr Cripps, Abraham Cooper

on keeping it. He said he must have horse exercise now that he's living in the country, and he's going to start riding tomorrow. He's ridden a few times in the Row on the animal that was accustomed to carry octogenarians and people undergoing rest cures, and that's about all his experience in the saddle—oh, and he rode a pony once in Norfolk, when he was fifteen and the pony twenty-four; and tomorrow he's going to ride the Brogue! I shall be a widow before I'm married, and I do so want to see what Corsica's like; it looks so silly on the map."

Clovis was sent for in haste, and the developments of the situation put before him.

"Nobody can ride that animal with any safety," said Mrs Mullet, "except Toby, and he knows by long experience what it is going to shy at, and manages to swerve at the same time."

"I did hint to Mr Penricarde—to Vincent, I should say— that the Brogue didn't like white gates," said Jessie.

"White gates!" exclaimed Mrs Mullet; "did you mention what effect a pig has on him? He'll have to pass Lockyer's farm to get to the high road, and there's sure to be a pig or two grunting about in the lane."

"He's taken rather a dislike to turkeys lately," said Toby.

"It's obvious that Penricarde mustn't be allowed to go out on that animal," said Clovis, "at least not till Jessie has married him, and tired of him. I tell you what: ask him to a picnic tomorrow, starting at an early hour; he's not the sort to go out for a ride before breakfast. The day after I'll get the rector to drive him over to Crowleigh before lunch, to see the new cottage hospital they're building there. The Brogue will be standing idle in the stable and Toby can offer to exercise it; then it can pick up a stone or something of the sort and go conveniently lame. If you hurry on the wedding a bit the lameness fiction can be kept up till the ceremony is safely over."

Mrs Mullet belonged to an emotional race, and she kissed Clovis.

It was nobody's fault that the rain came down in torrents the next morning, making a picnic a fantastic impossibility. It was nobody's fault, but sheer ill-luck, that the weather cleared up sufficiently in the afternoon to tempt Mr Penricarde to make his first essay with the Brogue. They did not get as far as the pigs at Lockyer's farm; the rectory gate was painted a dull unobtrusive green, but it had been white a year or two ago, and the Brogue never forgot that he had been in the habit of making a violent curtsey, a back-pedal and a swerve at this particular point of the road. Subsequently, there being apparently no further call on his services, he broke his way into the rectory orchard, where he found a hen turkey in a coop; later visitors to the orchard found the coop almost intact, but very little left of the turkey.

Mr Penricarde, a little stunned and shaken, and suffering from a bruised knee and some minor damages, good-naturedly ascribed the accident to his own inexperience with horses and country roads, and allowed Jessie to nurse him back into complete recovery and golf-fitness within something less than a week.

In the list of wedding presents which the local newspaper published a fortnight or so later appeared the following item:

"Brown saddle-horse, 'The Brogue', bridegroom's gift to the bride."

"Which shows," said Toby Mullet, "that he knew nothing."

"Or else," said Clovis, "that he has a very pleasing wit."

Robert Benchley, A Biography

Nathaniel Benchley

An incident symbolic of the lack of rapport between Robert Benchley and most animals occurred one time in Cambridge, when he was in college. Or possibly it shows great rapport; it is open to a wide variety of interpretations. At any rate, he and Paul Hollister were standing in front of Max Keezer's clothing store, in Harvard Square, and they happened to be discussing Lillian Russell, when Robert began to have the sensation of an extra presence in the conversation. Turning around, he saw that a policeman's horse, which had been standing at the curb, had edged up onto the sidewalk, and had its head practically on his shoulder. It was quietly breathing down his neck, apparently intent on catching every word he said.

Inquisitive Horse, Ming cloisonné

"Excuse me a minute," Robert said to Hollister, and he turned and faced the horse. "I was just saying," he said, "that Lillian Russell's opera company did more to make the American male conscious of music than any other single factor since Stephen Foster. Do you agree?"

The horse slowly shook its head.

"Good Lord, man, you must be mad," said Robert, just as an elderly lady walked past, stared, and then hurried on. "She possessed the rare combination of beauty and a good voice, the first of which drew men to see her and the second of which gave them musical pleasure to match their visual pleasure. Nobody in recent years has an appeal that anywhere near matches hers. Or perhaps you know of someone?"

The horse shook its head again, disregarding the small crowd that had begun to gather.

"Well, then," said Robert, "I see no point in continuing the argument. I'm perfectly willing to listen to a man who has the facts, but in the absence of them I think I am just wasting your time and mine. Come, Paul, let's get a malted."

He and Hollister walked away, and the horse stepped back into the street.

FROM

The Unvarnished West

J. M. Pollock

[In Texas, about 1880] I bought for $40 a little black horse of about $14\frac{1}{2}$ hands. He was handsome, quick and clever but full of tricks and as knowing as a monkey. One day while I was riding him over a flat piece of ground he got a cactus thorn in his foot and began to go very lame. I extracted the thorn, brought him slowly back to the ranch, and turned him out for a week, using meanwhile one of five or six other horses I owned. At the end of the week he was quite well and came in for a couple of days' pretty hard work. On starting out the third morning, he went dead lame. I caught another horse and turned Blackie loose. He ran off without showing the slightest lameness. The same thing happened on two or three other occasions, but I noticed that it was not always the same foot that he favored. One day after examining his foot carefully and finding nothing wrong, I continued my ride. He went very lame, first on one foot and then on another, but finally seeing that the trick was useless, gave it up, although with a very bad grace, and traveled well the rest of the day. He tried the dodge several times, till he found that it had no effect, and then gave it up for good. He had other tricks.

Jockeys horse-racing at Kalighat (Calcutta)

The Arab Tent, **Edwin Landseer**

The Adventures of
Baron Munchausen

R. E. Raspe

I set off from Rome on a journey to Russia, in the midst of winter, from a just notion that frost and snow must of course mend the roads, which every traveller has described as uncommonly bad through the northern parts of Germany, Poland, Courland and Livonia. I went on horseback, as the most convenient manner of travelling; I was but lightly clothed, and of this I felt the inconvenience the more I advanced north-east. What must not a poor old man have suffered in that severe weather and climate, whom I saw on a bleak common in Poland, lying on the road, helpless, shivering, and hardly having wherewithal to cover his nakedness? I pitied the poor soul: though I felt the severity of the air myself, I threw my mantle over him, and immediately I heard a voice from the heavens, blessing me for that piece of charity, saying—

"You will be rewarded, my son, for this in time."

I went on; night and darkness overtook me. No village was to be seen. The country was covered with snow, and I was unacquainted with the road.

Tired, I alighted, and fastened my horse to something like a pointed stump of a tree, which appeared above the snow; for the sake of safety I placed my pistols under my arm, and lay down on the snow, where I slept so soundly that I did not open my eyes till full daylight. It is not easy to conceive my astonishment to find myself in the midst of a village, lying in a churchyard; nor was my horse to be seen, but I heard him soon after neigh somewhere above me. On looking upwards I beheld him hanging by his bridle to the weathercock of the steeple. Matters were now very plain to me: the village had been covered with snow overnight; a sudden change of weather had taken place; I had sunk down to the churchyard whilst asleep, gently, and in the same proportion as the snow had melted away; and what in the dark I had taken to be a stump of a little tree appearing above the snow, to which I had tied my horse, proved to have been the cross or weathercock of the steeple!

Without long consideration I took one of my pistols, shot the bridle in two, brought down the horse, and proceeded on my journey.

The horse carried me well—advancing into the interior parts of Russia. But I found travelling on horseback rather unfashionable in winter, therefore I submitted, as I always do, to the custom of the country, took a single horse sledge, and drove briskly towards St. Petersburg. I do not exactly recollect whether it was in Eastland or Jugemanland, but I remember that in the midst of a dreary forest I spied a terrible wolf making after me, with all the speed of ravenous winter hunger. He soon overtook me. There was no possibility of escape. Mechanically I laid myself

The Polish Rider, Rembrandt van Rijn

down flat on the sledge, and let my horse run for our safety. What I wished, but hardly hoped or expected, happened immediately after. The wolf did not mind me in the least, but took a leap over me, and falling furiously on the horse began instantly to tear and devour the hind part of the poor animal, which ran the faster for his pain and terror. Thus unnoticed and safe myself, I lifted my head slyly up, and with horror I beheld that the wolf had eaten his way into the horse's body; it was not long before he had fairly forced himself into it, when I took my advantage, and fell upon him with the butt end of my whip. This unexpected attack in his rear frightened him so much that he leaped forward with all his might: the horse's carcass dropped on the ground, but in his place the wolf was in harness, and I on my part whipping him continually we both arrived in full career safe to St. Petersburg, contrary to our respective expectations, and very much to the astonishment of the spectators.

7

He Smelleth the Battle

Hast thou given the horse strength? hast thou clothed his neck with thunder? Canst thou make him afraid as a grasshopper? the glory of his nostrils is terrible. He paweth in the valley, and rejoiceth in his strength: he goeth on to meet the armed men.

He mocketh at fear, and is not affrighted; neither turneth he back from the sword. The quiver rattleth against him, the glittering spear and the shield. He swalloweth the ground with fierceness and rage; neither believeth he that it is the sound of the trumpet. He sayeth among the trumpets, Ha! Ha! and he smelleth the battle afar off, the thunder of the captains, and the shouting.

The Book of Job

The Lays of
Ancient Rome

Thomas Babington Macaulay

But north looked the Dictator,
   North looked he long and hard;
And spake to Caius Cossus,
   The captain of his guard:
"Caius, of all the Romans
   Thou hast the keenest sight;
Say, what through yonder storm of dust
   Comes from the Latian right?"

Then answered Caius Cossus:
   "I see an evil sight;
The banner of proud Tusculum
   Comes from the Latian right;
I see the plumed horsemen,
   And far before the rest
I see the dark-grey charger,
   I see the purple vest;
I see the golden helmet
   That shines far off like flame;
So ever rides Mamilius,
   Prince of the Latian name."

"Now hearken, Caius Cossus:
   Spring on thy horse's back;
Ride as the wolves of Apennine
   Were all upon thy track;
Haste to our southward battle:
   And never draw thy rein
Until thou find Herminius,
   And bid him come amain!"

Marcus Curtius, ascribed to Bacchiacca

So Aulus spake and turned him
    Again to that fierce strife;
And Caius Cossus mounted,
    And rode for death and life . . .
So he came far to southward,
    Where fought the Roman host
Against the banners of the marsh,
    And banners of the coast . . .

"Herminius, Aulus greets thee,
    He bids thee come with speed,
To help our central battle,
    For sore is there our need.
There wars the youngest Tarquin,
    And there the crest of flame,
The Tusculan Mamilius,
    Prince of the Latian name.
Valerius hath fallen fighting
    In front of our array,
And Aulus, of the seventy fields,
    Alone upholds the day."

Herminius beat his bosom:
    But never a word he spake,
He clapped his hand on Auster's mane:
    He gave the reins a shake,
Away, away, went Auster,
    Like an arrow from the bow:
Black Auster was the fleetest steed
    From Aufidus to Po.

Right glad were all the Romans
    Who, in that hour of dread,
Against great odds bore up the war
    Around Valerius dead,
When from the south the cheering
    Rose with a mighty swell;
"Herminius comes, Herminius,
    Who kept the bridge so well!"

Mamilius spied Herminius,
    And dashed across the way.
"Herminius, I have sought thee
    Through many a bloody day.
One of us two, Herminius,
    Shall never more go home.

I will lay on for Tusculum,
    And lay thou on for Rome!"

All round them paused the battle,
    While met in mortal fray
The Roman and the Tusculan,
    The horses black and grey.
Herminius smote Mamilius
    Through breast-plate and through breast;
And fast flowed out the purple blood
    Over the purple vest.
Mamilius smote Herminius
    Through head-piece and through head;
And side by side those chiefs of pride
    Together fell down dead.
Down fell they dead together
    In a great lake of gore,
And still stood all who saw them fall
    While men might count a score.

Fast, fast, with heels wild spurning,
    The dark grey charger fled:
He burst through ranks of fighting men;
    He sprang o'er heaps of dead.
His bridle far out-streaming,
    His flanks all blood and foam,
He sought the southern mountains,
    The mountains of his home.
The pass was steep and rugged,
    The wolves they howled and whined;
But he ran like a whirlwind up the pass,
    And he left the wolves behind.
Through many a startled hamlet
    Thundered his flying feet;
He rushed through the gate of Tusculum,
    He rushed up the long white street;
He rushed by tower and temple,
    And paused not from his race
Till he stood before his master's door
    In the stately market-place . . .

But, like a graven image,
    Black Auster kept his place,
And ever wistfully he looked
    Into his master's face.
The raven mane that daily,

A Battle, Johan van Hughtenburgh

With pats and fond caresses,
The young Herminia washed and combed,
  And twined in even tresses,
And decked with coloured ribands
  From her own gay attire,
Hung sadly o'er her father's corpse
  In carnage and in mire . . .
And Aulus the Dictator
  Stroked Auster's raven mane,
With heed he looked unto the girths,
  With heed unto the rein.
"Now bear me well, black Auster,
  Into yon thick array;
And thou and I will have revenge
  For thy good lord this day."

Apocalypse

D. H. Lawrence

Horses, always horses! How the horse dominated the mind of the early races, especially in the Mediterranean! You were a lord if you had a horse. Far back, far back in our dark soul the horse prances. He is a dominant symbol: he gives us lordship: he links us, the first palpable and throbbing link with the ruddy-glowing Almighty of potence: he is the beginning even of our godhead in the flesh. And as a symbol he roams the dark underworld meadows of the soul. He stamps and threshes in the dark fields of your soul and of mine. The sons of God who came down and knew the daughters of men and begot the great Titans, they had "the members of horses," says Enoch.

Within the last fifty years man has lost the horse. Now man is lost. Man is lost to life and power—an underling and a wastrel. While horses thrashed the streets of London, London lived.

The horse, the horse! the symbol of surging potency and power of movement, of action, in man. The horse, that heroes strode. Even Jesus rode an ass, a mount of humble power. But the horse for true heroes. And different horses for the different powers, for the different heroic flames and impulses.

The rider on the white horse! Who is he then? The man who needs an explanation will never know. Yet explanations are our doom.

Take the old four natures of man: the sanguine, the choleric, the melancholic, the phlegmatic. There you have the four colours of the horse, white, red, black, and *pale*, or yellowish. But how should sanguine be white?—Ah, because the blood was the life itself, the very life: and the very power of life itself was white, dazzling. In our old days, *the blood was the life*, and visioned as power it was like white light. The scarlet and the purple were only the clothing of the blood. Ah, the livid blood clothed in bright red! itself it was like pure light.

The red horse is choler; not mere anger, but natural fieryness, what we call passion.

The black horse was the black bile, refractory.

And the phlegm, or lymph of the body was the pale horse; in excess it causes death, and is followed by Hades.

Or take the four planetary natures of man: jovial, martial, saturnine and mercurial. This will do for another correspondence, if we go a little behind the Latin meaning, to the older Greek. Then Great Jove is the sun, and the living blood the white horse; and angry Mars rides the red horse; Saturn is black, stubborn, refractory and gloomy: and Mercury is really Hermes, Hermes of the Underworld, the guide of souls, the watcher over two ways, the opener of two doors, he who seeks through hell, or Hades.

Four Horsemen of the Apocalypse, Beatur of Liebana

There are two sets of correspondence, both physical. We leave the cosmic meanings, for the intention here is more physical than cosmic.

You will meet the white horse over and over again, as a symbol. Does not even Napoleon have a white horse? The old meanings control our actions, even when our minds have gone inert.

But the rider on the white horse is crowned. He is the royal me, he is my very self and his horse is the whole *mana* of a man. He is my very me, my sacred ego, called into a new cycle of action by the Lamb and riding forth to conquest, the conquest of the old self for the birth of a new self. It is he, truly, who shall conquer all the other "powers" of the self. And he rides forth, like the sun, with arrows, to conquest, but not with the sword, for the sword implies also judgment, and this

Death on a Pale Horse, Benjamin West

is my dynamic or potent self. And his bow is the bended bow of the body, like the crescent moon.

The true action of the myth, or ritual-imagery, has been all cut away. The rider on the white horse appears, then vanishes. But we know why he has appeared. And we know why he is paralleled at the end of the Apocalypse by the last rider on the white horse, who is the heavenly Son of Man riding forth after the last and final conquest over the "kings". The son of man, even you or I, rides forth to the small conquest; but the Great Son of Man mounts his white horse after the last universal conquest, and leads on his hosts.

Knight With Armour

Alfred Duggan

All over England knights were preparing for this pilgrimage. It was considered unwise for the English pilgrims to set out in a body; King William was nervous on his unstable throne, and would not let armed men gather together, for fear of another rebellion. As no great leader came forward in England to head the pilgrimage, and they did not all intend to follow the same lord, they crossed the Channel independently.

On the 1st of August 1096, the Feast of Saint Peter ad Vincula, Roger was ready to go. He and his two followers had taken the pilgrim's vow in the Abbey Church at Battle, and had sewn crosses of red cloth on the shoulders of their mantles as a visible sign of it.

The horses were in good condition. Jack, the warhorse, was ten years old, and considerably past his prime; but he was perfectly trained, ran straight at the mark without guidance from his rider, and, above all, could be trusted not to bolt in the charge, the most dangerous fault in a knight's warhorse. He was fat, but not too fat, and his wind and legs were still perfectly sound; he was a handsome, strong horse, chestnut with a white forehead and white socks, and his tail was long and flowing; that would have to be knotted up in battle, lest a footman catch hold of it to hamstring him, but it enhanced his appearance on the march. His fore-feet were shod, more as a weapon than as a protection against hard ground, but his hind-feet were bare. He led easily, was quiet with other horses, and knew both his rider and his groom. Of course, he was a stallion. On the march he would always wear his bridle, and the heavily-padded warsaddle, with its semicircular guardboards rising in front and behind to protect the rider's loins and waist. The heavy five-foot triangular shield would hang by its straps on the near side of the saddle; it was made of leather, stretched over a wooden framework, with a central boss of iron, and iron binding on the edges. It was a massive affair, much too heavy to be wielded by the left arm alone, and in action most of the weight was taken by a strap over the wearer's right shoulder, though he could direct it a little by movements of his bridle arm. Properly worn, it covered him from neck to ankle on the left side, and was proof against spears and arrows. Peter the Fleming, who led the warhorse, also carried the knightly lance, eight feet long and tipped with a sharp steel point. Lances had not yet become battering-rams, and the knight still tried to pierce his enemy in a vulnerable spot.

Godric led the baggage-horse. It was a sturdy pony from Devonshire, and carried its load in two large leather-covered panniers; these contained the best clothes of all three pilgrims, and Roger's supply of fresh linen. Balanced on top of the load was a light wooden cross the height of a man; the crosspiece was threaded through the sleeves of the mail shirt, and the hauberk and helm were fixed to the top. Godric carried a satchel for food and another for odds-and-ends, but he had to be watched lest he add these to the pony's load, or, worse still, climb on its back himself.

Carolingian Cavalry, 9th century

Roger rode the hackney, a common-looking brown beast, touched in the wind, but sound in all four legs; a verderer from Ashdown Forest had given it to him, as a personal contribution to the pilgrimage; it was quiet, with good paces, a comfortable ride for a long journey. Both hackney and baggage-horse were geldings, for greater ease of management in the crowd that was to be expected. Roger rode unarmed, in his second-best blue tunic, and thick blue cloth chausses, cross-gartered, but he wore his heavy, double-edged, blunt-ended sword to show that he was a knight.

So, on this first of August, they heard Mass and took Communion in the parish church of Ewhurst, and after breakfast set out on the dusty pack-road for Rye. Roger embraced his father and brother in the little cobbled courtyard of the hall, then mounted, with an unfamiliar tug at his left hip from the unaccustomed sword, and rode downhill to the long pile bridge over the tidal Rother. He knew that whatever happened in the future, whether he ruled as a rich baron in the unknown East, or died in vain among the mountains of the Sclavonians with nothing accomplished, he would never see Bodeham manor again, or any of his family. It was a depressing thought, but young men of eighteen look forward to the unknown, and he reflected that he was following the tradition of his race.

Military Campaign of Sultan Suleiman, 16th century

[165]

Rural Rides

William Cobbett

What a sight to behold soldiers, horse and foot, employed to prevent a distressed people from committing acts of violence, when the *cost* of the horse and foot would, probably, if applied in the way of relief to the sufferers, prevent the existence of the distress! A cavalry horse has, I think, ten pounds of oats a day and twenty pounds of hay. These at present prices cost 16s. a week. Then there is stable room, barracks, straw, saddle and all the trappings. Then there is the wear of the horse. Then the pay of them. So that one single horseman, with his horse, do not cost so little as 36s. a week; and that is more than the parish allowance to five labourers' or manufacturers' families, at five to a family; so that one horseman and his horse cost what would feed twenty-five of the distressed creatures. If there be ten thousand of these horsemen, they cost as much as would keep, at the parish rate, two hundred and fifty thousand of the distressed persons.

Germanic Horseman, 6th century

Love and the Loveless

Henry Williamson

Belton looked shabbier than when he had seen it in the spring. Much of the park and the surrounding grassland was now the colour of the soldiers' uniforms. Tens of thousands of feet and hooves and wheels had torn and discoloured the sward. Horses, riders, waggons, limbers, drivers, mules were daily in movement upon the landscape.

Having reported to "H" lines, he was sent to a troop, under a Riding Master, which was being formed that morning. With about a dozen other subalterns he was put in a section under a sergeant, who led the way to a hut, where, to Phillip's disappointment, they were told to seat themselves on forms for a lecture upon The Saddle.

He found no interest in this, so retired into the world of memory, hearing odd sentences across his mind-pictures.

"There are seven parts of the Saddle. They are, facing the horse's head, the Pommel, the Seat, the Cantle, the Flaps, Sweat Flaps, V-shape attachment, and Girth Tabs. The saddle should be placed in the centre of the horse's back, the front being one hand's-breadth from the play of the shoulder. Have you all got that down, gentlemen?"

No need to write it down, it's in the 2/- book I bought in Grantham, *Training for Transport Officers and Horsemanship*. If Desmond would only understand two things: that Lily had never really been his girl, because she did not love him; that he had never tried to get Lily for himself. Will it be any good if I write to Eugene, who was Desmond's friend first, and ask him to explain?

"The girth should lie flat and smooth around the horse's belly. It should admit one finger between it and the belly, the finger being placed in from the rear to the front, so that the hair is left lying in the right direction."

Pencils moved over note-books. Phillip sat withdrawn, mourning alone.

"If the hair is left ruffled under the girth, a girth-gall will be caused. The girth having been tightened by the straps provided, the surcingle should be placed over the saddle and girth and be as tight but no tighter than the girth. If the surcingle be tighter than the girth, the surcingle will rub and pinch the horse's skin, which would cause a most serious girth-gall."

He lived again the scene wherein Desmond had said that it would be best for everyone if he were killed. *You are too complicated a person to live.*

"The buckle of the surcingle should always be under the belly and in a direct line with the forelegs so as to escape rubbing the points of the elbows."

It would be no good writing to Eugene.

At the end of the hour a copy of *The Horse's Prayer* was given to each officer, a free issue from Our Dumb Friends League. Phillip glanced through it, and began to scoff inwardly, as he thought of the Riding School nags.

To Thee, my Master, I offer my prayer: Feed me, water and care for me, and, when the day's work is done, provide me with shelter, a dry clean bed and a stall wide enough for me to lie down in comfort.

Always be kind to me. Talk to me. Your voice often means as much to me as the reins. Gentle me sometimes, that I may learn to love you. Do not jerk the reins, and do not whip me when going up hill. Never strike, beat, or kick me when I do not understand what you want . . . watch me, and if I fail to do your bidding, see if something is wrong with my harness, or my feet . . . never put a frosty bit in my mouth . . . I often fall on the hard pavements which I have often prayed might not be of wood but of such a nature as to give me a safe and sure footing.

Remember that I must be ready at any moment to lose my life in your service.

He thought of the horses and mules lying beside the Harrow Road leading up to Loos: and the Dumb Friends League did not seem so funny.

And finally, O my Master, when my useful strength is gone, do not turn me out to starve or freeze, or sell me to some cruel owner, to be slowly starved and worked to death; but do Thou, my Master, take my life in the kindest way, and your God will reward you here and hereafter.

You will not consider me irreverent if I ask this in the name of Him who was born in a stable. Amen.

They left the hut and made their way to the picket lines, two long rows of horses tied to a rope and facing each other. Phillip had the same sergeant instructor as he had had during the spring; a sturdy, dark cavalryman, one of the original B.E.F. It seemed that the same old mounts were in use for the Riding School, too, a miscellaneous herd ranging between fifteen and seventeen hands high, hairies used to carrying awkward loads which usually began by patting their necks nervously, and continued the enforced relationship by speaking to them with two words only, *Whoa Back*, in tones of voice varying from confidential whisper to guttural threat. Nearly all the hairies were hard-mouthed from continual tuggings at the bits across their tongues, the curbed ends of which were chained around their lower jaws. Some horses, he knew, avoided this discomfort by working their bits forward between the teeth, so that a succession of booted rein-tuggers, their spur-rowels filed down for safety, and accustomed to handlebar steering, usually failed to elicit even a protesting shake of head, but only a continued neck-rigid boring as they sat forked, without balance, alarmingly high above the ground.

Before mounting, Phillip allowed the groom to show him what he knew already: the adjustment of stirrup leathers, by buckles under the saddle flaps, to the length of his arm from shoulder-pit to finger-tips. This equalled the length of leg, with heel well down, from boot to just above the knee.

"Prepare to mount! Mount!"

He was already familiar with the routine; and holding the reins in the approved manner through the fingers of his left hand, he pressed on the horse's withers while putting his left foot into the burnished iron. Then hopping up, he threw his right leg over the saddle and thrust the boot into the iron with one kick, thus completing mounting in one motion.

"I see you've ridden before, sir," remarked the sergeant, whose horse was standing nearby.

"You taught me, sergeant."

"I thought I recalled your face, sir."

Don Baltasar in the Riding School, Diego Velazquez

Sheridan's Ride

Thomas Buchanan Read

Up from the South at break of day,
Bringing to Winchester fresh dismay,
The affrighted air with a shudder bore,
Like a herald in haste to the chieftain's door,
The terrible grumble, and rumble, and roar,
Telling the battle was on once more,
And Sheridan twenty miles away.
And wider still those billows of war
Thundered along the horizon's bar;
And louder yet into Winchester rolled
The roar of that red sea uncontrolled,
Making the blood of the listener cold,
As he thought of the stake in that fiery fray,
And Sheridan twenty miles away.
But there is a road from Winchester town,
A good broad highway leading down;
And there, through the flash of the morning light,
A steed as black as the steeds of night
Was seen to pass as with eagle flight,
As if he knew the terrible need;
He stretched away with his utmost speed;
Hills rose and fell; but his heart was gay,
With Sheridan fifteen miles away.
Still sprung from those swift hoofs, thundering South,
The dust, like smoke from the cannon's mouth;
Or the trail of a comet, sweeping faster and faster,
Foreboding to traitors the doom of disaster.
The heart of the steed and the heart of the master
Were beating like prisoners assaulting their walls,
Impatient to be where the battle-field calls;
Every nerve of the charger was strained to full play,
With Sheridan only ten miles away.
Under his spurning feet the road
Like an arrowy Alpine river flowed,

And the landscape sped away behind,
Like an ocean flying before the wind,
And the steed, like a bark fed with furnace ire,
Swept on, with his wild eye full of fire.
But lo! he is nearing his heart's desire;
He is snuffing the smoke of the roaring fray,
With Sheridan only five miles away.
The first that the General saw were the groups
Of stragglers, and then the retreating troops;
What was done? what to do? a glance told him both,

An Episode on the Field of Battle, Charles-Philogène Tschaggeny

Then striking his spurs, with a terrible oath,
He dashed down the line, 'mid a storm of huzzas,
And the wave of retreat checked its course there, because
The sight of the master compelled it to pause.
With foam and with dust the black charger was gray;
By the flash of his eye, and the red nostrils' play,
He seemed to the whole great army to say,
"I have brought you Sheridan all the way
From Winchester, down to save the day."
Hurray! hurrah for Sheridan!
Hurrah! hurrah for horse and man!
And when their statues are placed on high
Under the dome of the Union sky,
The American soldiers' Temple of Fame,
There with the glorious General's name
Be it said in letters both bold and bright:
"Here is the steed that saved the day
By carrying Sheridan into the fight,
From Winchester—twenty miles away!"

8

Horse Loving

St Thomas says you cannot love a horse because it cannot love you back. This statement proved a serious obstacle to my entering the Holy Roman Church in 1948. Then Evelyn Waugh pointed out that St Thomas was an Italian accustomed to seeing his father's old chargers sent along to the local salami factory in Aquino. Had he been an English theologian he would never have written like that: his father's chargers would have been pensioned off in the park.

from Two Middle-Aged Ladies in Andalusia *by Penelope Chetwode*

Courser and Jennet

William Shakespeare

Courting Horses, 18th century porcelain

But, lo! from forth a copse that neighbours by,
    A breeding jennet, lusty, young, and proud,
Adonis' trampling courser doth espy,
    And forth she rushes, snorts and neighs aloud:
        The strong-necked steed, being tied unto a tree,
        Breaketh his rein, and to her straight goes he.

Imperiously he leaps, he neighs, he bounds,
    And now his woven girths he breaks asunder;
The bearing earth with his hard hoof he wounds,
    Whose hollow womb resounds like heaven's thunder;
        The iron bit he crusheth 'tween his teeth,
        Controlling what he was controlled with.

His ears up-pricked, his braided hanging mane,
  Upon his compassed crest now stand on end;
His nostrils drink the air, and forth again,
  As from a furnace, vapours doth he send:
    His eye, which scornfully glisters like fire,
    Shows his hot courage and his high desire.

Sometime he trots, as if he told the steps,
  With gentle majesty and modest pride;
Anon he rears upright, curvets and leaps,
  As who should say, "Lo! thus my strength is tried;
    And this I do to captivate the eye
    Of the fair breeder that is standing by."

What recketh he his rider's angry stir,
  His flattering "Holla", or his "Stand, I say"?
What cares he now for curb or pricking spur,
  For rich caparisons or trappings gay?
    He sees his love, and nothing else he sees,
    For nothing else with his proud sight agrees.

Look, when a painter would surpass the life,
  In limning out a well-proportioned steed,
His art with nature's workmanship at strife,
  As if the dead the living should exceed;
    So did this horse excel a common one,
    In shape, in courage, colour, pace and bone.

Round-hoofed, short-jointed, fetlocks shag and long,
  Broad breast, full eye, small head, and nostril wide,
High crest, short ears, straight legs and passing strong,
  Thin mane, thick tail, broad buttock, tender hide:
    Look, what a horse should have he did not lack,
    Save a proud rider on so proud a back.

Sometimes he scuds far off, and there he stares;
  Anon he starts at stirring of a feather;
To bid the wind a base he now prepares,
  And whether he run or fly they know not whether;
    For through his mane and tail the high wind sings,
    Fanning the hairs, who wave like feathered wings.

He looks upon his love, and neighs unto her;
  She answers him as if she knew his mind;
Being proud, as females are, to see him woo her,
  She puts on outward strangeness, seems unkind,

The Horses of Achilles, style of Van Dyck

Spurns at his love and scorns the heat he feels,
Beating his kind embracements with her heels.

Then, like a melancholy malcontent,
    He vails his tail that, like a falling plume,
Cool shadow to his melting buttock lent:
    He stamps, and bites the poor flies in his fume.
        His love, perceiving how he was enraged,
        Grew kinder, and his fury was assuaged.

His testy master goeth about to take him;
    When lo! the unbacked breeder, full of fear,
Jealous of catching, swiftly doth forsake him,
    With her the horse, and left Adonis there.
        As they were mad, unto the wood they hie them,
        Out-stripping crows that strive to over-fly them.

from Venus and Adonis

FROM

Don Quixote

Miguel de Cervantes Saavedra

The sage Cide Hamete Benengeli relates that as soon as Don Quixote had bidden farewell to his hosts and to everyone who had been present at the shepherd Chrysostom's burial, he and his squire entered that same wood into which they had seen the shepherdess Marcela disappear. And when they had travelled through it for more than two hours, looking for her in vain in all directions, they halted in a meadow, rich in fresh grass, beside which ran a pleasant and refreshing brook, which invited them, or rather induced them, to spend the sultry hours of midday there; for the heat had already become oppressive. Don Quixote and Sancho dismounted and, leaving the ass and Rocinante at large to feed on the abundant grass, they ransacked their saddle-bags. Then, without ceremony, master and man ate the contents in peace and good fellowship. Now Sancho had not troubled to fetter Rocinante, secure in his belief that he was so mild and so little lustful a beast that all the mares in the pastures of Cordova would not provoke

Don Quixote and Sancho Panza, Honoré Daumier

him to any impropriety. But as Fate, or the Devil—who is not always sleeping—would have it, there was a herd of Galician mares grazing in that valley. They belonged to some carriers from Yanguas whose habit it is to spend midday with their droves where there is grass and water; and the place where Don Quixote happened to be suited the Yanguesans very well. So it came about that Rocinante was taken with the desire to disport himself with the lady mares and, abandoning his natural pace and habits the moment he smelt them, asked no permission of his master, but set off at a brisk trot to acquaint them of his needs. But they, apparently, preferred the pastures, and gave him such a welcome with their hooves and teeth that in a very short while they had broken his girths and left him stripped of his saddle and naked. But what must have hurt him more was that the carriers, seeing the violence he was offering to their mares, ran up with pack-staves, and laid into him so hard that he was soon on the ground in a very sorry state. At this point Don Quixote and Sancho, who had witnessed Rocinante's beating, ran up panting, and the knight saying to his squire:

[179]

"From what I can see, friend Sancho, these are no knights, but vile and low-bred men. I say this so that you may freely help me to take due vengeance for the outrage which they have done to Rocinante before our very eyes."

"How the devil can we take revenge," replied Sancho, "when there are more than twenty of them, and we are only two—or perhaps no more than one and a half?"

"I am equal to a hundred," answered Don Quixote. Then without further discussion he drew his sword and attacked the Yanguesans; and Sancho Panza was spurred on by his master's example to do the same. At the first blow Don Quixote gave one of them a slash, which slit the leather coat he was wearing and cut a great gash in his shoulder. But the Yanguesans, seeing so many of themselves so roughly treated, by a mere two men, seized their pack-staves and, surrounding the pair, began to lay into them with might and main. In fact, they stretched Sancho on the ground at their second blow, and the same fate soon befell Don Quixote, his skill and courage availing him nothing; and, as Fate would have it, he fell at the feet of the still prostrate Rocinante. All of which goes to show what hard bruises pack-staves will deal in the hands of angry rustics. Then, seeing the damage they had done, the Yanguesans loaded their beasts as fast as they could and went on their way, leaving the two adventurers in an evil plight and a worse humour.

Translated from the Spanish by J. M. Cohen

The White Stallion

Pete Morgan

There was that horse
    that I found then
    my white one
big tall and lean as
    and mean as hell.

And people who saw me
    would stare as I passed them
    and say
        "Look at him . . .
    how he rides his cock-horse."

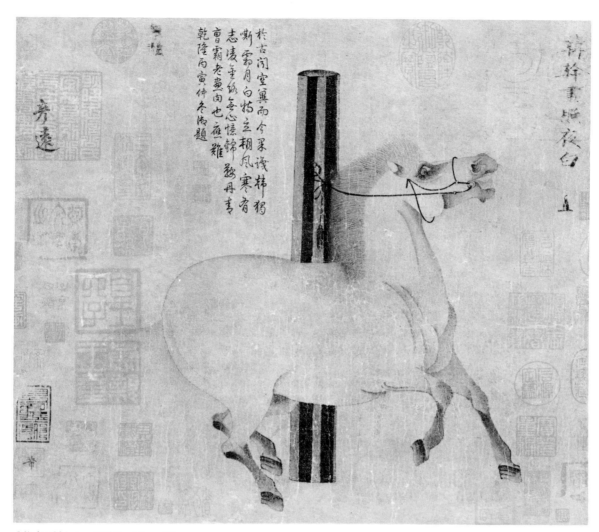

Night-Shining White, Han Kan

But my steed
   the white stallion
stormed into the moonlight
   and on it was me.

There were those girls
   that I found then
   my loved ones
small fat and lean ones
   and virgins as well.

[181]

And those girls who saw me
   would weep as I passed them
   and cry
      "Look at him . . .
   how he rides his cock-horse."

But my steed
   the white stallion
went proud in the still night
   and on it was me.

There was one girl
   that I loved then—
   a woman—
as tall and as lithe as
   a woman should be.

As soon as I saw her
   I dismounted my stallion
   to stay
      by the woman
   whose love I required.

But my steed
   the white stallion
rode off in the moonlight
   and on it was she.

Goodbye to the horse
   to the woman
   and stallion.
Farewell to my cock-horse
   and loving as well.

To people who see me
   and stare as I pass them
   I wail
      "Look at me . . .
   I once rode a cock-horse."

But my steed
   the white stallion
is lost in the moonlight
   and on it rides she.

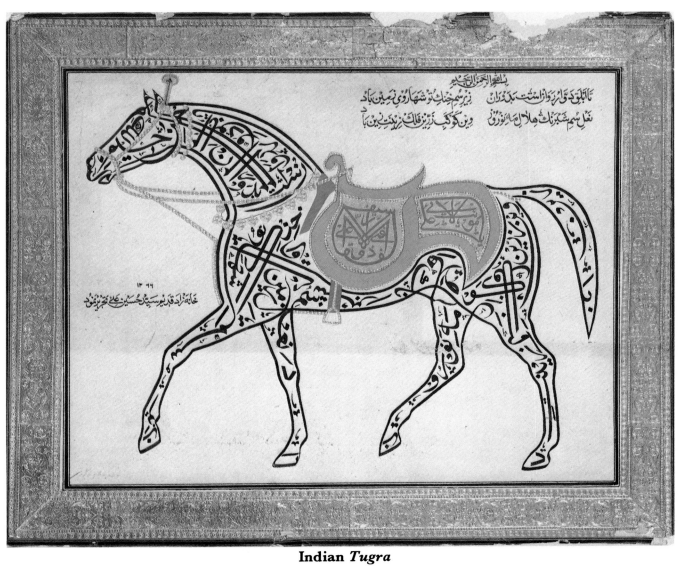

Indian *Tugra*

Rider, **Marino Marini**

Horse and Rider, Elizabeth Frink

9

Horse Triumphant

About the head of a truly great horse, there is an air of freedom unconquerable. The eyes seem to look on heights beyond our gaze. It is the look of a spirit that can soar. It is not confined to horses; even in his pictures you can see it in the eyes of the Bonaparte. It is the birthright of eagles.

John Taintor Foote

Napoleon Crossing the Alps, Jacques-Louis David

FROM

Moby Dick

Herman Melville

Most famous in our Western annals and Indian traditions is that of the White Steed of the Prairies; a magnificent milk-white charger, large-eyed, small-headed, bluff-chested, and with the dignity of a thousand monarchs in his lofty, over-scorning carriage. He was the elected Xerxes of the vast herds of wild horses, whose pastures in those days were only fenced by the Rocky Mountains and the Alleghanies. At their flaming head he westward trooped it like that chosen star which every evening leads on the hosts of light. The flashing cascade of his mane, the curving comet of his tail, invested him with housings more resplendent than gold- and silver-beaters could have furnished him. A most imperial and archangelical apparition of that unfallen western world, which to the eyes of the old trappers and hunters revived the glories of those primeval times when Adam walked majestic as a god, bluff-browed and fearless as this mighty steed. Whether marching amid his aides and marshals in the van of countless cohorts that endlessly streamed it over the plains, like an Ohio; or whether with his circumambient subjects browsing all around at the horizon, the White Steed gallopingly reviewed them with warm nostrils reddening through his cool milkiness; in whatever aspect he presented himself, always to the bravest Indians he was the object of trembling reverence and awe. Nor can it be questioned from what stands on legendary record of this noble horse, that it was his spiritual whiteness chiefly, which so clothed him with divineness; and that this divineness had that in it which, though commanding worship, at the same time enforced a certain nameless terror. . . .

Tell me, why this strong young colt, foaled in some peaceful valley of Vermont, far removed from all beasts of prey—why is it that upon the sunniest day, if you but shake a fresh buffalo robe behind him, so that he cannot even see it, but only smells its wild animal muskiness—why will he start, snort, and with bursting eyes paw the ground in frenzies of affright? There is no remembrance in him of any gorings of wild creatures in his green northern home, so that the strange muskiness he smells cannot recall to him anything associated with the experience of former perils; for what knows he, this New England colt, of the black bisons of distant Oregon?

No: but here thou beholdest even in a dumb brute, the instinct of the knowledge of the demonism in the world. Though thousands of miles from Oregon, still when he smells that savage musk, the rending, goring bison herds are as present as to the deserted wild foal of the prairies, which this instant they may be trampling into dust.

Horse Frightened by a Lion, George Stubbs

Florian the Lipizzaner

Felix Salten

Florian was going round the ring, sometimes with short steps, sometimes with raised knees and stretched forelegs. His milk-white, thick-set body somehow recalled the beauty of the naked human form; and as this subconscious association emerged one felt an impression of pure beauty, an exhilarating awareness of the perfect harmony of youth, strength and healthy vitality. Florian breathed hard and blew the froth from his mouth to the ground, where it lay in bright patches. As he moved he had a charming way of gently nodding his high-held head, rhythmically, as if the movement were timed to an inner music which he alone could hear.

Elizabeth and Neustift were enthusiastic. Their little son stared at Florian for a while and then exclaimed: "Mummy! he's singing . . . but you can't hear him!"

*   *   *   *   *

Anton was beginning to feel at home. He did not bother much about Vienna itself, but remained obstinately in the stables. If he had a free day he spent it with the horses or in the courtyard which, surrounded by the high buildings of the old castle, formed a little world of its own. It was Anton's world too. He was only too glad to ignore his opportunities of exploring beyond it. The outside world, the roaring life of the luxurious, fashionable city, the traffic and the gaiety, neither tempted him nor interested him. Beyond the archway lay for him an alien universe. His home was bounded by the gigantic walls of the Hofburg; within it Florian stood behind the bars of his loose box, and Bosco, too, was there. That sufficed him. Now and then he exchanged a short conversation with one of his colleagues. Anton was naturally laconic, and, like many men who are entirely devoted to the care of animals, he was reserved and even shy.

The sumptuous stable at first gave Anton a feeling of awestruck uneasiness. The costly brass-work which ornamented the wooden doors of the boxes and the luxurious appointments filled him with amazement. Each horse had a broad manger, into which a red marble trough was fitted, and each trough was supplied with running water from a tap above it. Superb harness hung on pegs before each compartment. The elegant tooled leatherwork displayed the imperial crown in gilt and sometimes the Emperor's initials as well. The horse-cloths of finest wool were piped with leather and fitted with buckles. The brushes and curry-combs were the best obtainable. There were bandages to protect the horses' eyes from being irritated by fragments of straw, and soft leather muzzles to prevent an animal from doing damage to a sore spot on its body or from removing the ointment with which the spot was being treated.

Anton learned to love the stable. The lofty smooth walls supported an arched ceiling. From a niche above each box a beautifully modelled horse's head looked down on the living animals below. Anton had no idea how many generations of noble steeds had been watched over by the silent heads above them. He knew nothing of Charles VI, who had founded the Spanish Riding School—he was completely ignorant of such things and rarely displayed curiosity about them. For aught he knew, the Hofburg had been standing there since time began; just as the Hapsburg Emperors had ruled Austria since time began: something which always had been and always would be. That was all he needed to know. For him and Florian the present was all that mattered. What the future held concerned him as little as the unknown past.

To reach the Riding School itself one had to cross the street which was spanned by the great archway. To Anton this street always seemed a profane, disturbing and obtrusive interlude. At times, though only for a few seconds, he was so bold as to wonder why the Emperor allowed people to make a thoroughfare through his house.

But the Riding School! When Anton entered it for the first time he stood at the entrance and put his hand over his mouth lest anyone should hear his exclamation: "Jesus Maria!" For a long time he stood as if in a church, sunk in profound reverence before this temple of the art of horsemanship.

The wide hall gave an impression of incredible height as the eye looked upwards to the roof. The dull ivory-white of the walls, the white embellishments of the balcony around, the pillared gallery above the balcony, borrowed a pleasing spaciousness from the sweep of the moulded ceiling, the ornamental balustrades and the daylight which streamed in from a double row of windows. The magnificent coat of arms which crowned the imperial box, the more than life-size picture of Charles VI on the main wall—Anton never had the courage to study closely the majestic splendour of these things. His gaze always became blurred, he felt himself humbled by the masterful power which the figures and emblems declaimed in their stony eloquence and impressive language.

It was for him a great event, perhaps the greatest in his life, when he was allowed to be present at a display in the Riding School. The riders, whom he had seen only in plain clothes hitherto, now wore gold-laced tail-coats of brown cloth, white, closely fitting buckskin knee-breeches and black patent-leather topboots. Their gloves were white, their stiffly curled white perukes were knotted with a black silk ribbon, and the two points of their cocked-hats projected over the ears.

The trappings of the horses, however, were plain and rich at once. The narrow reins were stamped with gilt. Midway along a thin strap across the chest of each horse hung a small glittering gold ornament like a rosette or a brooch. It vibrated and danced rather than hung, caressing and resplendent at the same time.

Anton watched as horses and riders took their places in the cavalcade. With a flourish of his cocked-hat each rider saluted the picture of Charles VI.

Then the display began.

Anton laughed. With his dumb, helpless grin he looked more than usually simple. Only the ecstatic glow in his eyes, his intense concentration on the scene before him, saved him from looking stupid. It was, rather, that the experience overpowered him. The supreme, the most perfect spectacle of horsemanship was being enacted before his eyes. He gazed at the almost miraculous unity of horse and rider, the incomprehensible harmony of animal and man. A stream of will, inflexible and pliant at once, merged with complete surrender to this will, a confident and loving obedience. The human nerves spoke in a wordless language to the alert nerves of the horse and received an immediate response. Anton was completely carried away. He had never dreamed that such a thing existed. When the name of the Spanish Riding School had been mentioned to him the words had gone in at one ear and out at the other; he had not even tried to form an idea of what they could mean.

Now it was all clear to him.

[191]

He grasped the meaning of the stud-farm at Lipizza, where he had served so long, of the extravagant luxury with which the Hofburg stables were equipped, and of the imposing majesty of the resplendent hall in which the white stallions from Lipizza were giving their wonderful performance. His fanatical ambition for Florian had hitherto lacked form and purpose. Now it had a definite and unmistakable aim. Anton walked about as if in a dream, or stood holding Florian's head in his arms and whispering into the alert, restless ears. "You can do it, Florian . . . far better than the others."

Translated from the German by Norman Gullick

The Spanish Pace, Johann Elias Ridinger

The Mustangs

Frank Dobie

Starface was a deep bay with a white star-shaped patch in his forehead and a stocking on his right forefoot. It was believed that he had Morgan blood in his veins; he might have been pure Spanish. In 1878 he was commanding a large band of mustangs that ranged between the Cimarron and Currumpa rivers in No Man's Land—the westward-pointing panhandle of Oklahoma. Every step that Starface took was a gesture of power and pride.

He would have been a marked horse anywhere, but his character made him even more noted than his carriage. He was the boldest gallant and the most magnificent thief that the Cimarron ranges had ever known. Most ranchmen in No Man's Land had horse herds as well as cattle and some raised horses altogether. Whenever Starface felt the blood stir in him, he would raid down upon these ranch horses, fight off the domestic stallions, cut out a bunch of mares with or without colts, and herd them back into his own well-trained bunch. The country was as yet unfenced, and Starface knew it all, claimed it all. He became a terror.

No man could walk him down, for Starface refused to circle. Nor could any man get near enough to crease him. Finally, the harassed ranchers organized to capture him. They took hundreds of long-distance shots at him; they cut off most of his followers; but he still ran free. Then they picked four cowboys, furnished them with the strongest and fastest horses in the country, and told them not to come back until they had killed or captured Starface. The four scouted for nearly a week before they sighted Starface's band. By keeping out of sight and riding in relays, they dogged the suspicious mustangs for three days and nights. Most of the time the cowboys kept back in the edge of the breaks on the south side of the Cimarron.

They studied the habits of mustangs as they had never studied them before. They marveled at the discipline by which the stallion kept his band in order. Now he would leave them and graze off alone, and not a mare would dare follow. Now he would round them into a knot that no yearling dared break from. Again he would course out with every animal obediently at his heels. Starface seemed to require less sleep than any other horse of the band.

It was early fall and the moon was in full quarter. Shortly after midnight on the fourth night the two cowboys on watch saw Starface leave his mares and head for the river flats. One man followed while his partner sped back to arouse their companions. A light dew on the grass made trailing easy; besides, the stallion was so intent on his quest that he seemed to pay no regard to what might be behind him. For six miles he galloped into the north.

Then, about ten miles east of the present town of Kenton, he entered a grassy canyon. Spreading out between walls of rock on either side, this canyon narrows into a chute that, in time of rains, pitches its waters off a bluff into the Cimarron River. Not far above the brink at the

Whistlejacket, George Stubbs

Horses in a Thunderstorm, Sawrey Gilpin

canyon mouth Starface passed through a narrow gateway of boulders shutting in a small valley.

Daylight was not far away when the cowboys came to the pass. They were familiar with the boxed structure of the canyon below them. They knew that Starface would before long be returning with his stolen mares. They decided to wait for him. They were sure that their opportunity had come. They were all determined to catch Starface rather than kill him, for studying him had changed vengeance into admiration.

In the early light they watched the bold stallion maneuvering about a dozen mares and colts. They were untrained to his methods, and Starface was wheeling and running in every direction, checking his captives at one point and whipping them up at another. Like a true master, he was intent on his business—and, for once, he was off guard.

He had worked the bunch into the pass, where the walls were hardly a hundred feet apart, and now the mares were stringing into discipline, when suddenly the four cowboys dashed from behind the boulders. Pistol shots shook the morning stillness. The wild Texas yell frenzied even the dullest of the mares. Ropes slapped against leather leggins and sang in the air.

With a wild snort of challenge, Starface charged alone up the steep canyon side. At first the cowboys thought he had discovered a trail out unknown to them. They stood still, watching, not a gun drawn. As the mustang ascended into a patch of sunshine allowed by a break in the walls on the opposite side of the canyon and they could see the sheen of light on his muscles, one of them called out, "God, look at the King of the horse world!" Long afterwards in describing the scene he added, "Not a man at that moment would have shot that animal for all the horses north of Red River."

But only for a brief time were they doubtful of capturing the superb stallion. They saw him leap to a bench as wide perhaps as a big corral—wide enough for a reckless cowboy to rope and manage an outlaw mustang upon. Towering above that bench was the caprock, without a seam or a slope in its face. Starface had picked the only spot at which the bench could be gained. But, like the canyon floor he had fled from, it ended in space—a sheer jump of ninety feet to the boulder-strewn bed of the Cimarron.

"Come on, we've got him," yelled one of the mustangers.

Under the excitement, the horses they were riding leaped up the way the mustang had led. Now he was racing back and forth along the bench. As the leading rider emerged to the level, he saw Starface make his last dash.

He was headed for the open end of the bench. At the brink he gathered his feet as if to vault the Cimarron itself, and then, without halting a second, he sprang into space. For a flash of time, without tumbling, he remained stretched out, terror in his streaming mane and tail, the madness of ultimate defiance in his eyes. With him it was truly "Give me Liberty or give me Death."

The Black Mare

Liam O'Flaherty

I bought the mare at G———, from a red-whiskered tinker and, if the truth were only known, I believe he stole her somewhere in the south, for he parted with her for thirty shillings. Or else it was because she was so wild that there was not another man at the whole fair had the courage to cross her back with his legs and trot her down the fair green but myself, for it was not for nothing that they called me Dan of the Fury in those days. However, when I landed from the hooker at the pier at Kilmurrage and, mounting her, trotted up to the village, they all laughed at me. For she was a poor-looking animal that day, with long shaggy hair under her belly, and the flesh on her ribs was as scarce as hospitality in a priest's house. She didn't stand an inch over fourteen hands, and my legs almost touched the ground astride of her. So they laughed at me, but I paid no heed to them. I saw the fire in her eyes, and that was all I needed. You see this drop of whiskey in this glass, stranger? It is a pale, weak colour, and it would not cover an inch with wetness, but it has more fire in it than a whole teeming lake of soft water. So the mare.

The Racehorse Manuella, John Frederick Herring Senior

I set her to pasture in a little field I had between two hills in the valley below the fort. I cared for her as a mother might care for an only child, and all that winter I never put a halter in her mouth or threw my legs across her back, but I used to watch her for hours galloping around the fields snorting, with her great black eyes spitting fire and her nostrils opened so wide that you could hide an egg in each of them. And, Virgin of the Valiant Deeds, when she shed her winter coat in spring and I combed her glossy sides, what a horse she was! As black as the sloes they pick on the slope of Coillnamhan Fort, with never a hair of red or white or yellow. Her tail swept to the ground, and when the sun shone on her sides you could see them shimmering like the jewels on a priest's vestments; may the good God forgive me, a sinner, for the comparison. But what is nearer to God than a beautiful horse? Tell me that, stranger, who have been in many lands across the sea.

And then the day came when all the unbroken mares of Inverara were to be shod. For it was the custom then, stranger, to shoe all the young mares on the same day, and to break them before they were shod on the wide sandy beach beneath the village of Coillnamhan.

[197]

There were seven mares that day gathered together from the four villages of Inverara, and there were good horses among them, but none as good as mine. She was now a little over fifteen hands high, and you could bury a child's hand between her haunches. She was perfect in every limb, like a horse from the stable of the God Crom. I can see her yet, stranger, standing on the strand stamping with her hind leg and cocking her ears at every sound. But it's an old saying, talk of beauty today, talk of death tomorrow.

I kept her to the last, and gave her to a lad to hold while I mounted a bay mare that my cousin had brought from Kilmillick, and I broke her in three rounds of the strand, although she had thrown three strong and hardy men before I seized her halter. And then my mare was brought down, and then and there I offered three quarts of the best whiskey that could be bought for money to the man that could stay on her back for one length of the strand. One after the other they mounted her, but no sooner did they touch her back than she sent them headlong to the ground. She would gather her four legs together and jump her own height from the ground, and with each jump they flew from her back, and she would run shivering around again until they caught her. I smiled, sitting there on a rock.

Then Shemus, the son of Crooked Michael, spat on his hands, tightened his crios around his waist, and said that if the devil were hiding in her bowels and Lucifer's own step-brother riding on her mane, he would break her. He was a man I never liked, the same son of Crooked Michael, a braggart without any good in him, a man who must have come crooked from his mother's womb, and his father before him was the same dishonest son of a horse-stealing tinker. "Be careful," I said to him; "that mare is used to have men about her that didn't drink their mother's milk from a teapot." And when I saw the ugly look he gave me I knew that there was trouble coming, and so there was.

Man and Horse, I, Elizabeth Frink

Soldier on a Horse, Michel Larionov

White Horse and Sleeping Man, Andrew Murray

He got up on her all right, for, to give the devil his due, he was agile on his limbs and, although no horseman, there were few men in the island of Inverara that he couldn't throw with a twist of the wrist he had. But as soon as his legs rubbed her flanks she neighed and gathered herself together to spring, and just as she was that way doubled up he kicked her in the mouth with his foot. She rose to her hind legs and before she could plant her fore feet on the ground again to jump, I had rushed from the rock and with one swing of my right arm I had pulled him to the ground. I was so mad that before he could rush at me I seized him by the thigh and the back of the neck, and I would have broken every limb in his putrid body if they didn't rush in and separate us. Then the craven son of a reptile that he was, as soon as he saw himself held, he began to bellow like a young bull wanting to get at me. But I took no heed of him. My father's son was never a man to crow over a fallen enemy.

They brought the mare over to me and I looked at her. She looked at me, and a shiver passed down her flank and she whinnied, pawing the sand with her hind hoof.

"Take off that halter," said I to the men.

They did. I still kept looking at the mare and she at me. She never moved. Then coming over to her as she stood there without saddle or bridle, stepping lightly on my toes, I laid my right hand on her shoulder. "Pruach, pruach, my beautiful girl," I called to her, rubbing her shoulders with my left hand. Then I rose from the strand, leaning on the strength of my right hand and landed on her back as lightly as a bird landing on a rose bush. She darted forward like a flash of lightning from a darkened sky. You see that strand, stretching east from the rock to where it ends in a line of boulders at the eastern end. It is four hundred paces and it rises to the south of the boulders into a high sand bank underneath the road. Well, I turned her at the sand bank with a sudden flash of my hand across her eyes, leaning out over her mane. And then back again we came, with a column of sand rising after us and the ground rising up in front of us with the speed of our progress. "Now," said I to myself, "I will show this son of Crooked Michael what Dan of the Fury can do on horseback."

Raising myself gently with my hands on her shoulders, I put my two feet square on her haunches and stood straight, leaning against the wind, balancing myself with every motion of her body, and as she ran, stretched flat with her belly to earth, I took my blue woollen shirt off my back and was down again on her shoulders as light as a feather before we reached the western end, where the men stood gaping as if they had seen a priest performing a miracle. "God be with the man," they cried. And the women sitting on the hillock that overlooks the beach screamed with fear and enjoyment, and of all the beautiful women that were gathered there that day there was not one that would not have been glad to mate with me with or without marriage.

Back over the strand again we went, the black mare and I, like lightning flying from the thunder, and the wave that rose when we passed the rock in the west had not broken on the strand when we turned again at the sand bank. Then coming back again like the driven wind in winter I rose once more, standing on her haunches, and may the devil swallow me alive if I hadn't put my shirt on my back again and landed back on her shoulders before we reached the rock. There I turned her head to the sea and drove her out into it until the waves lapped her heaving belly. I brought her back to the rock as gentle as a lamb and dismounted.

Ha! My soul from the devil, but that was a day that will never be forgotten as long as there is a man left to breathe the name of Dan of the Fury. But all things have their end, and sure it's a queer day that doesn't bring the night, and the laugh is the herald of the sigh. It was two years after that I got this fractured thigh. Well I remember that four days before the races where I got this broken limb, I met red-haired Mary of Kilmillick. As I was looking after her, for she had shapely hips and an enticing swing in them, my horse stumbled, and although I crossed myself

The Race, Conrad Seckmann

three times and promised to make a journey to the Holy Well at Kilmillick, I'll swear by Crom that the spell of the Evil One was put on the mare. But that is old woman's talk. Mary promised me the morning of the races that if the black mare won, I could put a ring on her finger, and as I cantered up to the starting point I swore I would win both the race and the girl if the devil himself were holding on to the black mare's tail.

Seventeen horses lined up at the starting point. I took up my position beside a bay stallion that the parish priest, Fr John Costigan, had entered. He was a blood stallion and had won many races on the mainland, but the parish priest was allowed to enter him, for who could go against a priest. Then, as now, there was nobody in Inverara who was willing to risk being turned into a goat by making a priest obey the rules of a race. Six times they started us and six times we were forced to come back to the starting point, for that same braggart, the son of Crooked Michael, persisted in trying to get away before the appointed time. At last the parish priest knocked him off his horse with a welt of his blackthorn stick and the race started.

We were off like sixteen claps of thunder. We had to circle the field three times, that big field above the beach at Coillnamhan, and before we had circled it the second time, the bay stallion and the mare were in front with the rest nowhere. Neck to neck we ran, and no matter how I urged the mare she would not leave the stallion. Then in the third round of the field I caught a sight of Mary looking at me with a sneer on her face, as if she thought I was afraid to beat the priest's horse. That look drove me mad. I forgot myself. We were stretching towards the winning post. The stallion was reaching in front of me. Mad with rage I struck the mare a heavy blow between the ears. I had never struck her in my life and as soon as I had done it I started with fright and shame. I had struck my horse. I spoke to her gently but she just shivered from the tip of her ears to her tail and darted forward with one mighty rush that left the stallion behind.

I heard a shout from the people. I forgot the blow. I forgot the mare. I leaned forward on her mane and yelled myself. We passed the winning post, with the stallion one hundred yards or more behind us. I tried to draw rein. Her head was like a firm rock. I cursed her and drew rein again. I might have been a flea biting her back. At one bound she leapt the fence and swept down the beach. She was headed straight for the boulders. I saw them in front of me and grew terrified. Between us and the boulders was the sand bank, fifteen feet high. She snorted, raised her head and tried to stop when she saw the fall. I heard a shout from the people. Then I became limp. We rose in the air. We fell. The mare struck the rocks and I remembered no more.

They told me afterward that she was shattered to a pulp when they found us, and sure it's the good God that only gave me a broken leg.

How They Brought the Good News from Ghent to Aix

Robert Browning

I sprang to the stirrup, and Joris, and he;
I galloped, Dirck galloped, we galloped all three;
"Good speed!" cried the watch, as the gate-bolts undrew;
"Speed!" echoed the wall to us galloping through;
Behind shut the postern, the lights sank to rest,
And into the midnight we galloped abreast.

Not a word to each other: we kept the great pace
Neck by neck, stride by stride, never changing our place;

Officer of the Light Cavalry, Théodore Géricault

I turned in my saddle and made its girths tight,
Then shortened each stirrup, and set the pique right,
Rebuckled the cheek-strap, chained slacker the bit,
Nor galloped less steadily Roland a whit.

'Twas moonset at starting; but while we drew near
Lokeren, the cocks crew and twilight dawned clear;
At Boom, a great yellow star came out to see;
At Düffeld, 'Twas morning as plain as could be;
And from Mecheln church-steeple we heard the half-chime,
So Joris broke silence with, "Yet there is time!"

At Aershot, up leaped of a sudden the sun,
And against him the cattle stood black every one,
To stare thro' the mist at us galloping past,
And I saw my stout galloper Roland at last,
With resolute shoulders, each butting away
The haze, as some bluff river headland its spray.

And his low head and crest, just one sharp ear bent back
For my voice, and the other pricked out on his track;
And one eye's black intelligence,—ever that glance
O'er its white edge at me, his own master, askance!
And the thick heavy spume-flakes which aye and anon
His fierce lips shook upwards in galloping on.

By Hasselt, Dirck groaned; and cried Joris, "Stay spur!
Your Roos galloped bravely, the fault's not in her,
We'll remember at Aix"—for one heard the quick wheeze
Of her chest, saw the stretched neck and staggering knees,
And sunk tail, and horrible heave of the flank,
As down on her haunches she shuddered and sank.

So we were left galloping, Joris and I,
Past Looz and past Tongres, no cloud in the sky;
The broad sun above laughed a pitiless laugh,
'Neath our feet broke the brittle bright stubble like chaff;
Till over by Dalhem a dome-spire sprang white,
And "Gallop," gasped Joris, "for Aix is in sight!"

"How they'll greet us!"—and all in a moment his roan
Rolled neck and croup over, lay dead as a stone;
And there was my Roland to bear the whole weight
Of the news which alone could save Aix from her fate,
With his nostrils like pits full of blood to the brim,
And with circles of red for his eye-sockets' rim.

[203]

Then I cast loose my buffcoat, each holster let fall,
Shook off both my jack-boots, let go belt and all,
Stood up in the stirrup, leaned, patted his ear.
Called my Roland his pet-name, my horse without peer;
Clapped my hands, laughed and sang, any noise, bad or good,
Till at length into Aix Roland galloped and stood.

And all I remember is, friends flocking round
As I sat with his head 'twixt my knees on the ground;
And no voice but was praising this Roland of mine,
As I poured down his throat our last measure of wine,
Which (the burgesses voted by common consent)
Was no more than his due who brought good news from Ghent.

FROM

Wild Fire

Zane Grey

The weird lights magnified the wild stallion and showed him clearly. He seemed gigantic. He shone black against the fire. His head was high, his mane flying. Behind him the fire flared and the valley-wide column of smoke rolled majestically upward, and the great monuments seemed to retreat darkly and mysteriously as the flames advanced beyond them. It was a beautiful, unearthly spectacle, with its silence the strangest feature.

But suddenly Wild Fire broke that silence with a whistle which to Slone's overstrained faculties seemed a blast as piercing as the splitting sound of lightning. And with the whistle Wild Fire plunged up towards the pass.

Slone yelled at the top of his lungs and fired his gun before he could terrorize the stallion and drive him back down the slope. Soon Wild Fire became again a running black object, and then he disappeared.

The great line of fire had got beyond the monuments and now stretched unbroken across the valley from wall to slope. Wild Fire could never pierce that line of flames. And now Slone saw, in the paling sky to the east, that dawn was at hand.

Looking grimly glad, with the first red flash of sunrise, Slone felt a breeze fan his cheek. All that was needed now was a west wind. And here came the assurance of it as he gazed before him.

White Horse Frightened by a Storm, Eugène Delacroix

The valley appeared hazy and smoky, with slow, rolling clouds low down where the line of fire moved. The coming of daylight paled the blaze of the grass, though here and there Slone caught flickering glimpses of dull red flame. The wild stallion kept to the centre of the valley, restlessly facing this way and that, but never towards the smoke. Slone made sure that Wild Fire gradually gave ground as the line of smoke slowly worked towards him.

Every moment the breeze freshened, grew steadier and stronger, until Slone saw that it began to clear the valley of the low-hanging smoke. There came a time when once more the blazing line extended across from slope to slope.

Wild Fire was cornered, trapped. Many times Slone nervously uncoiled and recoiled his lasso. Presently the great chance of his life would come—the hardest and most important throw he would ever have with a rope. He did not miss often, but he missed sometimes—and here he must be swift and sure.

It annoyed him that his hands perspired and trembled and that something weighty seemed to obstruct his breathing. He was pretty much worn out, not in the best of condition for a hard fight with a wild horse. Slone was prepared for hours of strained watching, and then a desperate effort, and then a shock that might kill Wild Fire and cripple Nagger, or a long race and fight.

But he soon discovered that he was wrong about the long watch and wait. The wind had grown strong and was driving the fire swiftly. The flames, fanned by the breeze, leaped to a formidable barrier. In less than an hour Wild Fire had been driven down towards the narrowing neck of the valley, and he had begun to run, to and fro, back and forth.

Wild Fire showed evidence of terror, but he did not attempt to make the pass. Instead he went at the righthand slope of the valley and began to climb. The slope was steep and soft, yet the stallion climbed up and up. The dust flew in clouds; the gravel rolled down, and the sand followed in long streams.

"Go ahead, you red devil!" yelled Slone. He was much elated. In that soft bank Wild Fire would tire out while not hurting himself.

Slone watched the stallion in admiration and pity and exultation. Wild Fire did not make much headway, for he slipped back almost as much as he gained. He attempted one place after another. The slope above was endless and grew steeper, more difficult towards the top. Slone knew absolutely that no horse could climb over it. He grew apprehensive, however, for Wild Fire might stick up there on the slope until the line of fire passed.

Long sheets of sand and gravel slid down to spill thinly over the low bank. Wild Fire, now sinking to his knees, worked steadily upwards till he had reached a point halfway up the slope, at the head of a long, yellow bank of treacherous-looking sand. Here he was halted by a low bulge, which he might have surmounted had his feet been free. But he stood deep in the sand. For the first time he looked down at the sweeping fire, and then at Slone.

Suddenly the bank of sand began to slide with him. He snorted in fright. The avalanche started slowly and was evidently no mere surface slide. It was deep. It stopped—then started again—and again stopped. Wild Fire appeared to be sinking deeper and deeper. His struggling only embedded him more firmly. Then the bank of sand, with an ominous roar, began to move once more. This time it slipped swiftly.

The Broken Rope, Charles M. Russell

Just as suddenly the avalanche stopped again. Slone saw, from the great oval hole it had left before, that it was indeed deep. That was the reason it did not slide readily. When the dust cleared away Slone saw the stallion, sunk to his flanks in the sand, utterly helpless.

With a wild whoop Slone leaped off Nagger, and, a lasso in each hand, ran down a quarter of a mile distant, and, since the grass was thinning out, it was not coming so fast as it had been. The position of the stallion was halfway between the fire and Slone, and a hundred yards up the slope.

Like a madman Slone climbed up through the dragging, loose sand. He was beside himself with a fury of excitement. In his eagerness he slipped, and fell, and crawled, and leaped, until he reached the slide which held Wild Fire prisoner.

The stallion might have been fast in quicksand up to his body for all the movement he could make. He could move only his head. He held that up, his eyes wild, showing the whites, his foaming mouth wide open, his teeth gleaming.

As Slone leaped within roping distance the avalanche slipped a foot or two—halted—slipped once more, and slowly started again with that low roar. He leaped closer, whirling his rope. The loop hissed round his head and whistled as he flung it. And when fiercely he jerked back on the rope, the noose closed tight round Wild Fire's neck.

"By—God—I—got—a rope—on him!" cried Slone in hoarse pants.

Wild Fire's head seemed a demon-head of hate. It reached out, mouth agape, to bite, to rend.

Then came the moment of triumph for Slone. No moment could ever equal that one, when he realized he stood there with a rope around that grand stallion's neck. All the days and the miles and the toil and the endurance and the hopelessness and the hunger were paid for in that moment. His heart seemed too large for his breast.

"I tracked—you!" he cried savagely. "I stayed—with you! An' I got a rope—on you! An'—I'll ride you—you red devil!"

He hauled on the lasso, pulling the stallion's head down and down. The action was the lust of capture as well as the rider's instinctive motive to make the horse fear him.

The avalanche slipped with little jerks, as if treacherously loosing its hold for a long plunge. The line of fire below ate at the bleached grass and the long column of smoke curled away on the wind.

Slone held the taut lasso with his left hand, and with the right he swung the other rope, catching the noose round Wild Fire's nose. Then letting go of the first rope he hauled on the other, pulling the head of the stallion far down. Hand over hand Slone closed in on the horse. He leaped on Wild Fire's head, pressed it down, and, holding it down on the sand with his knees, in a hackamore. Then, just as swiftly, he bound his scarf tight round Wild Fire's head, blindfolding him.

"All so easy!" exclaimed Slone under his breath. "Lord! Who would believe it! Is it a dream?" He rose and let the stallion have a free head.

The avalanche had begun to slide, to heave and bulge and crack. Dust rose in clouds from all around. The sand appeared to open and let him sink to his knees. The rattle of gravel was drowned in a soft roar.

Then he shot down swiftly, holding the lassos, keeping himself erect, and riding as if in a boat. He felt the successive steps of the slope, and then the long incline below, and then the checking and rising and spreading of the avalanche as it slowed down on the level. All movement then was checked violently. He appeared to be half buried in sand. While he struggled to extricate himself the thick dust blew away and settled so that he could see.

Wild Fire lay before him, at the edge of the slide, and now he was not so deeply embedded as he had been up on the slope. He was struggling and probably soon would have been able to get out. The line of fire was close now, but Slone did not fear that.

At his shrill whistle Nagger bounded towards him, obedient, but snorting, with ears laid back. He halted. A second whistle started him again. Slone finally dug himself out of the sand, pulled the lassos out, and ran the length of them towards Nagger.

"Come on!" called Slone harshly. He got a hand on the horse, pulled him round, and, mounting in a flash, wound both lassos round the pommel of the saddle.

"Haul him out, Nagger, old boy!" cried Slone, and he dug spurs into the black.

One plunge of Nagger's slid the stallion out of the sand. Snorting, wild, blinded, Wild Fire got up, shaking in every limb. He plunged, rearing at the end of the plunge, and struck out viciously with his hooves.

Slone, quick with spur and bridle, swerved Nagger aside and Wild Fire, off his balance, went down with a crash. Slone dragged him, stretched him out, pulled him over twice before he got forefeet planted. Once up he reared again, screeching his rage, striking wildly with his hooves. Slone wheeled aside and toppled him over again.

Again he dragged the stallion. He was ruthless. He would have to be so, stopping just short of maiming or killing the horse, else he would never break him. But Wild Fire was nimble. He got to his feet and this time he lunged out. Nagger, powerful as he was, could not sustain the tremendous shock, and went down. Slone saved himself with a rider's supple skill, falling clear of the horse, and he leaped again into the saddle as Nagger bounded up. Nagger braced his huge frame and held the plunging stallion. But the saddle slipped a little; the cinches cracked. Slone eased the strain by wheeling after Wild Fire.

The horses had worked away from the fire, and Wild Fire, free of the stifling smoke, began to break and lunge and pitch, plunging round Nagger in a circle, running blindly. Slone avoided the rushes, making a pivot of Nagger round which the wild horse dashed in his frenzy.

"Steady, Nagger, old boy!" Slone kept calling. "He'll never get at you—if he slips that blinder I'll kill him!"

The stallion was a fiend in his fury, quicker than a panther, wonderful on his feet, and powerful as an ox. But he was at a disadvantage. He could not see. The soft sand in the pass was ploughed deep before Wild Fire paused in his mad plunges. He was wet and heaving.

Slone uncoiled the lassos from the pommel and slacked them a little. Wild Fire stood up, striking at the air, snorting fiercely. Slone tried to wheel Nagger in close behind the stallion. Both narrowly escaped the vicious hooves. Slone took a desperate chance and spurred Nagger in a single leap as Wild Fire reared again. The horses collided. Slone hauled the lassos tight. The impact threw Wild Fire off his balance, just as Slone had calculated, and as the stallion plunged down on four feet Slone spurred Nagger close against him.

Wild Fire was a little in the lead. He could only half-rear now, for Nagger, always against him, jostled him down, and Slone's iron arm hauled on the short ropes. When Wild Fire turned to bite, Slone knocked the vicious nose back with a long swing of his fist.

Up the pass the horses plunged. Slone saw the long green-and-gray valley, and the isolated monuments in the distance.

"Run, you red devil!" Slone called. "Drag us around now till you're done!"

They left the pass and swept out upon the waste of sage. Slone realized, from the stinging of the sweet wind in his face, that Nagger was being pulled at a tremendous pace. The faithful black could never have made the wind cut so. Lower the wild stallion stretched and swifter he ran, till it seemed to Slone that death must end that thunderbolt race.

10

Cavalcade Through the Ages

Then, in my vision, heaven opened, and I saw a white horse appear. Its rider bore for his title, the Faithful, the True; he judges and goes to battle in the cause of right. His eyes were like flaming fire, and on his brow were many royal diadems; the name written there is one that only he knows. He went clad in a garment deep dyed with blood, and the name by which he is called is the Word of God; the armies of heaven followed him, mounted on white horses, and clad in linen, white and clean.

The Revelation of St John the Divine

FROM

Plutarch's Lives

Two Horsemen, from west frieze of the Parthenon

Philonicus the Thessalian brought the horse Bucephalus to Philip, offering to sell him for thirteen talents; but when they went into the field to try him, they found him so very vicious and unmanageable, that he reared up when they endeavoured to mount him, and would not so much as endure the voice of any of Philip's attendants. Upon which, as they were leading him away as wholly useless and untractable, Alexander, who stood by, said, "What an excellent horse do they lose for want of address and boldness to manage him!" Philip at first took no notice of what he said; but when he heard him repeat the same thing several times, and saw he was much vexed to see the horse sent away, "Do you reproach," said he to him, "those who are older than yourself, as if you knew more, and were better able to manage him than they do?" "I could manage this horse," replied he, "better than others do." "And if you do not," said Philip, "what will you forfeit for your rashness?" "I will pay," answered Alexander, "the whole price of the horse." At this the whole company fell a-laughing; and as soon as the wager was settled amongst them, he immediately ran to the horse, and taking hold of the bridle, turned him directly towards the sun, having, it seems, observed that he was disturbed at and afraid of the motion of his own shadow; then letting him go forward a little, still keeping the reins in his hands, and stroking him gently when he found him begin to grow eager and fiery, he let fall his upper garment softly, and with one nimble leap securely mounted him, and when he was seated, by little and little drew in the bridle, and curbed him without either striking or spurring him. Presently, when he found him free from all rebelliousness, and only impatient for the course, he let him go at full speed, inciting him now with a commanding voice, and urging him also with his heel. Philip and his friends

[211]

looked on at first in silence and anxiety for the result, till seeing him turn at the end of his career, and come back rejoicing and triumphing for what he had performed, they all burst out into acclamations of applause; and his father shedding tears, it is said, for joy kissed him as he came down from his horse and in his transport said, "O my son, look thee out a kingdom equal to and worthy of thyself, for Macedonia is too little for thee."

FROM

Legends of Charlemagne

Thomas Bulfinch

Rinaldo was one of the four sons of Aymon, who married Aya, the sister of Charlemagne. Thus Rinaldo was nephew to Charlemagne and cousin of Orlando.

When Rinaldo had grown old enough to assume arms, Orlando had won for himself an illustrious name by his exploits against the Saracens, whom Charlemagne and his brave knights had driven out of France. Orlando's fame excited a noble emulation in Rinaldo. Eager to go in pursuit of glory, he wandered in the country near Paris, and one day saw at the foot of a tree a superb horse, fully equipped and loaded with a complete suit of armor. Rinaldo clothed himself in the armor and mounted the horse, but took not the sword. On the day when, with his brothers, he had received the honor of knighthood from the Emperor, he had sworn never to bind a sword to his side till he had wrested one from some famous knight.

Rinaldo took his way to the forest of Arden, celebrated for so many adventures. Hardly had he entered it, when he met an old man, bending under the weight of years, and learned from him that the forest was infested with a wild horse, untamable, that broke and overturned everything that opposed his career. To attack him, he said, or even to meet him, was certain death. Rinaldo, far from being alarmed, showed the most eager desire to combat the animal. This was the horse Bayard, afterwards so famous. He had formerly belonged to Amadis of Gaul. After the death of that hero, he had been held under enchantment by the power of a magician, who predicted that, when the time came to break the spell, he should be subdued by a knight of the lineage of Amadis, and not less brave than he.

To win this wonderful horse, it was necessary to conquer him by force or skill; for from the moment when he should be thrown down, he would become docile and manageable. His habitual resort was a cave on the borders of the forest; but woe be to any one who should approach him, unless gifted with strength and courage more than mortal. Having told this, the old man departed. He was not, in fact, an old man, but Malagigi, the enchanter, cousin of Rinaldo, who,

Knights Jousting, from L'Histoire d'Alexandre Le Grand

to favor the enterprises of the young knight, had procured for him the horse and armor which he so opportunely found, and now put him in the way to acquire a horse unequalled in the world.

Rinaldo plunged into the forest, and spent many days in seeking Bayard, but found no traces of him. One day he encountered a Saracen knight, with whom he made acquaintance, as often happened to knights, by first meeting him in combat. This knight, whose name was Isolier, was also in quest of Bayard. Rinaldo succeeded in the encounter, and so severe was the shock that Isolier was a long time insensible. When he revived, and was about to resume the contest, a peasant who passed by (it was Malagigi) interrupted them with the news that the terrible horse was near at hand, advising them to unite their powers to subdue him, for it would require all their ability.

Rinaldo and Isolier, now become friends, proceeded together to the attack of the horse. They found Bayard, and stood a long time, concealed by the wood, admiring his strength and beauty.

A bright bay in color (whence he was called Bayard), with a silver star in his forehead, and his hind feet white, his body slender, his head delicate, his ample chest filled out with swelling muscles, his shoulders broad and full, his legs straight and sinewy, his thick mane falling over his arching neck,—he came rushing through the forest, regardless of rocks, bushes, or trees, rending everything that opposed his way, and neighing defiance.

He first descried Isolier, and rushed upon him. The knight received him with lance in rest, but the fierce animal broke the spear, and his course was not delayed by it for an instant. The Spaniard adroitly stepped aside, and gave way to the rushing tempest. Bayard checked his career,

[213]

Month of May, from Les Tres Riches Heures du duc de Berry, Pol de Limbourg

and turned again upon the knight, who had already drawn his sword. He drew his sword, for he had no hope of taming the horse; that, he was satisfied, was impossible.

Bayard rushed upon him, fiercely rearing, now on this side, now on that. The knight struck him with his sword, where the white star adorned his forehead, but struck in vain, and felt ashamed, thinking that he had struck feebly, for he did not know that the skin of that horse was so tough that the keenest sword could make no impression upon it.

[214]

Whistling fell the sword once more, and struck with greater force, and the fierce horse felt it, and drooped his head under the blow, but the next moment turned upon his foe with such a buffet that the Pagan fell stunned and lifeless to the earth.

Rinaldo, who saw Isolier fall, and thought that his life was reft, darted towards the horse, and with his fist, gave him such a blow on the jaws that the blood tinged his mouth with vermilion. Quicker than an arrow leaves the bow the horse turned upon him, and tried to seize his arm with his teeth.

The knight stepped back, and then, repeating his blow, struck him on the forehead. Bayard turned, and kicked with both his feet with a force that would have shattered a mountain. Rinaldo was on his guard, and evaded his attacks, whether made with head or heels. He kept at his side, avoiding both; but, making a false step, he at last received a terrible blow from the horse's foot, and at the shock almost fainted away. A second such blow would have killed him, but the horse kicked at random, and a second blow did not reach Rinaldo, who in a moment recovered himself. Thus the contest continued until by chance Bayard's foot got caught between the branches of an oak. Rinaldo seized it, and putting forth all his strength and address, threw him on the ground.

No sooner had Bayard touched the ground, than all his rage subsided. No longer an object of terror, he became gentle and quiet, yet with dignity in his mildness.

The paladin patted his neck, stroked his breast, and smoothed his mane, while the animal neighed and showed delight to be caressed by his master. Rinaldo, seeing him now completely subdued, took the saddle and trappings from the other horse, and adorned Bayard with the spoils.

Rinaldo became one of the most illustrious knights of Charlemagne's court.

FROM

The Cloister and The Hearth

Charles Reade

My servant, the count, finding me curious, took me to the stables of the prince that rules this part. In the first court was a horse bath, adorned with twenty-two pillars, graven with the prince's arms; and also the horse-leech's shop, so furnished as a rich apothecary might envy. The stable is a fair quadrangle, whereof three sides filled with horses of all nations. Before each horse's nose was a glazed window, with a green curtain to be drawn at pleasure, and at his tail a thick wooden pillar with a brazen shield, whence by turning of a pipe he is watered, and serves too for a

The Royal Stables, at Chantilly, 1874

cupboard to keep his comb and rubbing cloths. Each rack was iron, and each manger shining copper, and each nag covered with a scarlet mantle, and above him his bridle and saddle hung, ready to gallop forth in a minute; and not less than three hundred horses, whereof twelve score of foreign breed.

And we returned to our inn full of admiration, and the two varlets said sorrowfully, "Why were we born with two legs?" And one of the grooms that was civil and had of me trinkgeld, stood now at his cottage door, and asked us in. There we found his wife and children of all ages, from five to eighteen, and had but one room to bide and sleep in, a thing pestiferous and most uncivil. Then I asked my servant, knew he this prince? Ay, did he, and had often drunk with him in a marble chamber above the stables, where, for table, was a curious and artificial rock, and the drinking vessels hang on its pinnacles, and at the hottest of the engagement a statue of a horseman in bronze came forth bearing a bowl of liquor, and he that sat nearest behooved to drain it. "'Tis well," said I: "now, for the penance; whisper thou in yon prince's ear that God hath given him his people freely, and not sought a price for them as for horses. And pray him look inside the huts of his horse-palace door, and bethink himself is it well to house his horses and stable his folk." Said he, "'Twill give sore offence." "But," said I, "ye must do it discreetly, and choose your time." So he promised. And riding on we heard plaintive cries. "Alas," said I, "some sore mischance hath befallen some poor soul; what may it be?"

[216]

Stable Interior, George Morland

FROM

Sartor Resartus

Thomas Carlyle

The Horse I ride has his own whole fell; strip him of girths and flaps and other extraneous tags that I have fastened round him, and the noble creature is his own sempster and weaver and spinner, nay, his own bootmaker, jeweller, and man-milliner; he bounds free through the valleys, with a perennial rain-proof Court suit on his body, wherein warmth, and easiness of fit, have reached perfection; and frills and fringes, with gay variety of colour, featly appended, and ever in the right place, are not wanting.

While I—good Heaven! have thatched myself over with the dead fleeces of sheep, the bark of vegetables, the entrails of worms; the hides of seals or oxen, the felt of furred beasts, and walk about—a moving Rag-Screen!

A Highland Scene, Edwin Landseer

Grapes and Granite

Nina Epton

The most famous of all the *arrapa das bestas* that take place in Galicia is to be seen at San Lorenzo of Sabucedo, whose church must be the only one in the world to own a herd of wild horses. In the beginning, and nobody knows how long ago that was, San Lorenzo owned a herd of cattle, but the bubonic plague wiped them out, as well as most of the congregation. Two elderly and panic-stricken spinsters of the parish decided to build themselves a hut on the mountain about a mile away from the village and to offer a couple of horses to the good San Lorenzo if they were spared from the disease. The spinsters survived, the plague disappeared, and the two horses let loose in the hills multiplied until in the course of time they came to be known as "San Lorenzo's herd". There is still a hut in the woods known locally as the "old ladies' house", which is pointed out to strangers in support of the traditional story.

Nowadays the herd is an economic institution; proceeds of sales go to church funds and all are under the exalted supervision of the prelates of Compostela, who nominate the "governing body", presided over by the parish priest of Sabucedo, which is responsible for the various operations.

Not all the wild horses that roam over Mount Montouto belong to the saint, however. Some two or three hundred of them belong to private individuals and only a hundred or so bear the mark, in the shape of a grid, that indicates their connexion with the parish's patron saint (who was martyred on a grid). The San Lorenzo horses are divided into twelve groups, each under the leadership of a separate stallion. These horses are small and sturdy, with thick manes and powerful muscles, capable of withstanding extremes of temperature and long periods of under-nourishment. They are the result of interbreeding between the ancient *celdones* and the *asturcones*, or small horses of northern Spain, and they are said to be as resistant as the horses of Siberia, China and the Himalayas.

These herds cover great distances in search of fresh pastures and during their treks they occasionally encounter other groups who try to prevent them from crossing into their territory. Dramatic battles take place between the leading stallions in which even the mares sometimes take part. When the stallion from each rival group advances to meet its rival, battle is waged until one of the two gives in and is chased away by the victor. The mares of the vanquished sire abandon the battle at the same time but, far from being faithful to their master in adversity, they usually follow the superior new lord who has proved stronger and braver than the old one.

When the stallions begin to grow old, their position in the herd is disputed by the hot-blooded young beaux, who from their third spring begin to make amorous advances to the mares. These first timid efforts are spurned by the mares but they do not pass unheeded by the father, who

Broodmares and Colts in a Landscape, Sawrey Gilpin and George Barret

immediately declares war upon the colts until they are forced to leave the herd. They are sometimes accompanied in their exile by their mother and sisters and a young girl-friend, while the sire remains surrounded by the faithful. Little by little, the colt builds up his own herd, until the day comes when the patriarch dies or becomes incapable of exercising his functions, and then all the mares accept the new lord and master without question.

At other times, when the mares are on heat, the old stallions are provoked by colts of from four to six years old who try to steal their herd from them. The old stallion begins to fight back with all the *maîtrise* he has developed over the years. The colts are more agile and quicker in their movements, but they lack technique. Age, however, soon takes its toll. The stallion's teeth have been slowly filed down by the prickly mountain furze for countless seasons and now they can hardly bite at all, while the colt's young teeth are as sharp as nails and pierce his flesh unmercifully.

The patriarch rises bravely on to his hind legs, but they are no longer as steady as they used to be and soon he sways, loses his balance and falls upon his back, usually sustaining a fatal injury to his spinal column. His rival is generous enough to desist from attacking him while he is lying helpless and disconsolate and gallops off, leaving his vanquished elder alone and humiliated. The cycle is complete. When he was young, he had done the same. Now it is his turn to give way. There is nothing more to expect from life. Even in those cases where the aged stallion survives his fall, he is broken in spirit. His paces are slow and uncertain, his once lordly neigh is replaced by a pitiful lament; from then on, his days are numbered. The mares remain with him until he falls never to rise again. Sometimes quite a long while elapses before they are convinced that their master is well and truly dead and they continue to graze near the corpse until a new stallion takes them under his wing.

When news reaches the parish of Sabucedo that an old stallion has been killed in battle with a younger rival, all the villagers feel genuinely sad and for a long time afterwards they are filled with hatred for the victor.

The herds have diminished in numbers through the effect of illness and thefts, but the cruellest plague of all is the mountain wolf, who attacks not only the foals but also the weakest among the mares. No healthy wild mare is afraid of a wolf, for whom she is more than a match,

Spring on the Range, American School

so the wolf resorts to the following wily stratagem: first of all, the wolf looks for a pool or marsh in which it wallows until it is covered with mud. Then, very cautiously, it approaches its intended victim, waits for her to adopt an attitude of defence, creeps up close and shakes itself violently to blind her with mud. The mare instinctively raises her head to avoid being spattered, and the instant she does so, the wolf seizes her by the neck and holds on tenaciously until, her arteries having been severed, she dies from loss of blood. Several wolves usually band together for an attack of this nature, otherwise the stallion would undoubtedly come to the mare's rescue.

The peasants of San Lorenzo look forward for weeks to the annual "fiesta of the mountain horses". The fun starts on Whit Sunday at five in the morning, when the church bells of Sabucedo announce the Mass of the Holy Ghost, which is attended by all those who are to take an active part in the day's proceedings.

After Mass the men assemble with their sticks and baskets of refreshments before leaving for the mountains to round up the horses. Hundreds of people from neighbouring villages accompany them on their arduous climb.

A little after six o'clock in the evening, the herds are brought down into Sabucedo (this phase of the proceeding is known as the *abaixada*). The horses are then placed in a compound where they spend the night under the supervision of a specially appointed night-watchman, and at nine o'clock the dancing starts in the village square. Wine flows freely, bagpipes play, and the fun goes on until the small hours of the morning.

On the Monday, at six in the morning, the horses are carefully counted and the privately owned animals are separated from church property. All the colts of from one to three years are marked prior to their sale; after this the newly born foals are marked. This operation is performed by the village boys under the guidance of grown-ups, to acquaint them with the ways of wild horses.

At eleven in the morning, the horses are taken to the *corro*, in which the actual *rapa* or cutting of manes takes place in the middle of an indescribable medley of noise, dust, confusion and merriment, with the horses kicking and neighing and biting in all directions.

Once the herds are all well inside the *corro*, they put their heads together as if they were about to be attacked by wolves. Then the stallions begin to fight. The peasants, even the children, elbow their way fearlessly between them all to rescue the foals, who risk being trampled or kicked to death in the stampede. (The foals are let loose after the *rapa*, on the Monday, when the herds set off again for their mountain home; in no time the little creatures find their respective mothers and trot contentedly by their sides, bound for the wild, windblown moors.)

Once the foals have been taken out of the *corro*, the expert cutting of manes begins. The peasants, armed with long sticks, charge through the heaving mass of excited beasts, shouting and gesticulating and pushing the animals tightly against one another; this is where the *agarradores* come into their own.

First, one of them selects a horse whose mane he intends to cut, springs like a tiger upon its prey, clinging on as best he can, with one hand clutching the horse's neck or mane while he hammers blows on its ears with the other to make it dizzy; then, stretching himself full length upon its back, he passes one hand over the animal's forehead and takes hold of its jaw, pressing its head upon its chest; while he is thus engaged, another *agarrador* holds the horse by pushing his fingers up its nostrils or sitting astride its neck, at the same time seizing the opposite jaw to the one his colleague is holding, so that between them, with their arms crossed in front of the horse's eyes, they keep him blindfolded.

While the two *agarradores* hold the horse by the head, two others hold it by the tail, tweaking it firmly from one side to the other to prevent it from rearing. The horse bucks and tries every trick it knows to force itself free from its aggressors, but sheer weariness eventually compels it to give up. At this moment the horse is separated from the rest, placed in a corner or against one of the walls of the *corro*, while the cutters with their long scissors proceed to trim the mane and tail. The horsehair is placed in sacks, ready to be sold by auction later on in the day to the many buyers who gather from all parts of the province for the occasion. Half of the horses are dealt with on the Monday and the remaining half on the Tuesday. Private owners cut the manes and tails of their horses in their homes.

Four *agarradores* usually suffice to hold a horse down, but very often, in the case of the valiant fighting stallions, as many as eight men are needed on the job. These *agarradores* are necessarily young men aged between twenty and twenty-five. Many of them are as famous locally as the top-grade bullfighters of Madrid and Seville.

Taking Wild Horses in Moldavia, Samuel Howitt

Tschiffely's Ride

A. F. Tschiffely

A few words on the origin of the Creole horse may show the reasons for their powers of resistance. They are the descendants of a few horses brought to the Argentine in 1535 by Don Pedro Mendoza, the founder of the city of Buenos Aires. These animals were of the finest Spanish stock, at that time the best in Europe, with a large admixture of Arab and Barb blood in their veins. That these were the first horses in America is borne out by history, by tradition, and by the fact that no native American dialect contains a word for horse. Later, when Buenos Aires was sacked by the Indians and its inhabitants massacred, the descendants of the Spaniards' horses were abandoned to wander over the country. They lived and bred by the laws of nature, they were hunted by the Indians and wild animals, drought would compel them to travel enormous distances in search of water, the treacherous climate with its sudden changes of temperature killed off all but the strongest, and, in short, they were forced to obey the natural law of "survival of the fittest". The fitness of the race has been amply proved. During the War of Emancipation and the various Indian wars, the Creole horses performed marches that would appear incredible were it not an established fact. Dr Solanet, in an admirable speech delivered at a conference of the Agricultural and Veterinary Faculties, said: "Their marches for months during the War of Emancipation are not reckoned by kilometres but by leagues: a hundred, two hundred and more was the distance frequently covered in these wonderful raids, which terminated at the ranks of the Spanish soldiers, valiant it cannot be denied, since they are of our own race. And the horses of the Patriots arrived with sufficient energy to drive home a victorious charge. Afterwards, the same night, they would rest, feeding on whatever they could 'rustle'. Without covering they endured frosts, and on the following day, instead of massage and grooming, came the violent hot gale that scorched them and lashed them with burning sand."

The two horses given to me by Dr Solanet were "Mancha", who was at the time sixteen years old, and "Gato", who was fifteen. They had formerly been the property of a Patagonian Indian Chief named Liempichun ("I have feathers") and were the wildest of the wild. To break them in had been a task that taxed the powers of several of the best *domadores* for some time, and even when I took them over they were far from tame. I may state that even now (at twenty-two years of age) after a journey of over ten thousand miles, Mancha will not allow anyone except myself to saddle him. These two animals had, a very short time previously, come up to the *estancia* with a troop from Patagonia and had performed a road march of over a thousand miles, in the course of which they had lived on what they could find, which was not much. To a European horse-lover they would appear, to put it mildly, curious. Mancha is a red, with heavy irregular splashes of white; white face and stockings. In the U.S. and in England this colour is sometimes called

Two Horses, Delftware

"pinto" or "piebald". Gato is more or less of a coffee colour, a sort of a cross between a bay and a dun, or what the American cowboys used to call a "buckskin". Their sturdy legs, short thick necks and Roman noses are as far removed from the points of a first-class English hunter as the North Pole from South. "Handsome is as handsome does," however, and I am willing to state my opinion boldly that no other breed in the world has the capacity of the Creole for continuous hard work. The horses obtained, there still remained many other points to be considered, primarily the question of riding and of pack saddles. For riding I chose the type of saddle used in Uruguay and the northern parts of Argentina. This consists of a light framework, about two feet long, over which is stretched a covering of hide. This sits easily on the horse, and, being covered with loose sheep-skins, makes a comfortable bed at night, the saddle forming the pillow. I used the same saddle throughout the trip, but was obliged to change the pack saddle in the mountainous regions. To take a tent was, of course, an impossibility, owing to the weight, so I had to be content with a large poncho (cloak) for covering when sleeping out. A big mosquito-net in the shape of a bell tent was taken, as it folded up into a very small space and weighed practically nothing.

I then had to spend several weeks getting into riding condition and accustoming myself to long expeditions. As a schoolmaster I had had perforce to be content with riding during vacations and consequently a considerable amount of practice was necessary.

When the preparations were nearly complete, the horses were sent up to Buenos Aires and lodged in the fine premises of the Argentine Rural Society. This was not easy. Let the reader imagine the feelings of two savage warriors from the interior of Africa suddenly dumped into Piccadilly or Broadway. The nearest approach to a town that either of them had seen was an Indian village composed of a few toldos—tents made of posts and raw hide. To bring them across the city, which was done in the early hours of the morning and by the least frequented streets, and finally to persuade them to enter the stables was a labour worthy of Hercules himself. The very streets and houses scared them, while an automobile!! They turned up their noses at the most luscious alfalfa, barley, oats, etc, with which they were provided and devoured with relish the straw put down for bedding. In this respect, however, they soon changed, and began to realise what was good, and, as they gradually filled out on good fodder, so did their spirits, none too tame before, rise, and exercising them became a really interesting, not to say exciting job.

Ponies on a Welsh Hillside, David Jones

Aesop's Fables

In ancient times, when the Horse and the Deer ranged the forest with uncontrolled freedom, it happened that contentions arose between them about grazing in particular meadows. These disputes ended in a conflict between them, in which the Deer proved victorious, and with his sharp horns drove the Horse from the pasture. Full of disappointment and chagrin, the Horse applied to the Man, and craved his assistance, in order to re-establish him in the possession of his rights. The request was granted, on condition that he would suffer himself to be bridled, saddled, and mounted by his new ally, with whose assistance he entirely defeated his enemy; but the poor Horse was mightily disappointed when, upon returning thanks to the Man, and desiring to be dismissed, he received this answer: No, I never knew before how useful a drudge you were; now I have found what you are good for, you may be assured I will keep you to it.

A Horse with a Saddle Nearby, Abraham van Calraet

Old Gray Mare

Oh, the old gray mare, she ain't what she used to be,
Ain't what she used to be, ain't what she used to be.
The old gray mare she ain't what she used to be,
    Many long years ago.
Many long years ago, many long years ago,
The old gray mare, she ain't what she used to be,
    Many long years ago.

The Garden of Eden (detail), Jan Breughel

The old gray mare, she kicked on the whiffletree,
Kicked on the whiffletree, kicked on the whiffletree.
The old gray mare she kicked on the whiffletree,
    Many long years ago.
Many long years ago, many long years ago,
The old gray mare, she ain't what she used to be,
    Many long years ago.

from Carl Sandburg's The American Song-bag

FROM

Ambrose's Vision

Giles Gordon

Ambrose's eye was attracted by a gleam of light in the landscape, some distance from the cathedral. A silver fleck in the verdant tapestry. The sun had caught a tin can, or something of the sort, a bit of silver paper even, maybe discarded by a child from a bar of chocolate.

He gave it not a further thought until a few minutes later a knight on horseback, as if straight out of Dürer, came clopping by. At this time, this period of European history, after the ravages of the word and the world, of years of fighting—moral and physical—between the forces of good and the forces of evil, and not either side always being sure which it was, knights in full armour going through the discipline of chivalry were comparatively rare. Rare enough for heads to turn and stare, for eyebrows to be raised and the odd titter emitted; to wonder if the person on horseback really was a knight, or someone playing the goat, or a daredevil child romanticising olden times.

Clip clop, he went, the man on horseback. Clip clop clop. Whether the sound was made by the horse or the man was debatable. They were trying to hold together, person and horse, an unnatural centaur.

The knight, or figure on horseback, reined in his steed—though nag would have been a more appropriate epithet—close to the cathedral. Ambrose didn't recognise the surcoat or coat of arms but then he wouldn't have expected to have done. He'd left his heraldry manual at home, not having anticipated this encounter. He stood at the door of his cathedral, the west front, as if an innkeeper, mine host, or even an ostler expecting to be handed the horse or what remained of it.

[229]

A Knight, Death and the Devil, Albrecht Dürer

He nodded minimally up at the rider, in such a way that the gesture could not positively be construed either as greeting or servility but as one or the other depending upon how the horseman felt inclined to react.

Said the knight, having removed his helmet and shown the stubble on his chin: "I'm in search of the holy grail."

Aren't we all, thought Ambrose, whether we know it or not. But the man had spoken in such a way, such a tone of voice, that Ambrose believed that the piss was not being taken, that this was for real, or at least that the man—the knight—thought it was. And to think of it as real is to be real, to be participating in the mighty quest.

He looked down, the knight did, from his great height. Not that he was seven feet tall but that mounted on his horse he seemed twice the height of grounded Ambrose. His face was young and eager, blue eyes, blond hair, an archetypal grail hunter. Though his journey had been long and exhausting, the body within the face that shone out quite clearly retained its sparkle, its sense of mission, of purpose.

Ambrose realised that there was an opportunity here to capitalise on something, that this chance encounter could—in the most honourable way—be turned to advantage. He would gain, and so would Sir Knight. He, Ambrose, or the cathedral, the combination of Ambrose and cathedral, could become an appendage to legend, Ambrose as Merlin, Ambrose as Arthur, the cathedral as round table, as Camelot.

He asked the knight (for there was no doubt in his mind, having seen the face, that the rider was a knight) to dismount, to do him the honour of entering his cathedral.

Procession of the Magi, Benozzo Gozzoli

His cathedral? thought the knight. Here's a conceited fellow. Still, that was not his problem, it was the fellow's. He slid off his horse, and he and Ambrose entered the cathedral.

Ambrose tried to explain what he had in mind, having assumed that the knight would have known. The knight was incredulous:

"Tomato juice? For God's sake . . ."

Ambrose was taken aback by the reaction:

"But it's a legend, my dear chap."

I am not part of a legend, thought the knight. I am part of life, I am myself. Quite deranged, this fellow; quite deranged. Not to say blasphemous.

"You mean to say . . .?" said the knight, he doing the saying, yet not being able to articulate a response. Wine, blood, tomato juice. They're all red, and there has to be something in the pot, the casket. That was what Ambrose had been saying, explaining, speculating. It *looked* like wine in the chalice Ambrose had shown him but it hadn't smelt like wine, or frankly like tomato juice.

The knight wheeled away from the sight, from the altar, insofar as his armour permitted him freedom of movement.

"No. No. No," he shouted, louder and louder, more and more hysterically. He clattered down the aisle with Ambrose following close behind. What an idiot, he thought. What a waste.

The holy fool came out of the west front, from darkness to light or so he saw it and was dazzled, transfixed by the sun striking his armour. The quest was what he was about, not the discovery. In the legend (and here he was succumbing to his own mythology) the grail was not found.

His horse knew that he would be mounted again, that the journey would continue. There was his master, still lacking that thing he searched the world for. If horses could think, thought the horse; if horses could talk, the things that horses would think and tell.

The Horses

Edwin Muir

Barely a twelvemonth after
The seven days war that put the world to sleep,
Late in the evening the strange horses came.
By then we had made our covenant with silence,
But in the first few days it was so still
We listened to our breathing and were afraid.

Four Galloping Horses, Raymond de la Fage

On the second day
The radios failed; we turned the knobs; no answer.
On the third day a warship passed us, heading north,
Dead bodies piled on the deck. On the sixth day
A plane plunged over us into the sea. Thereafter
Nothing. The radios dumb;
And still they stand in corners of our kitchens,
And stand, perhaps, turned on, in a million rooms
All over the world. But now if they should speak,
If on a sudden they should speak again,
If on the stroke of noon a voice should speak,
We would not listen, we would not let it bring
That old bad world that swallowed its children quick

At one great gulp. We would not have it again.
Sometimes we think of the nations lying asleep,
Curled blindly in impenetrable sorrow,
And then the thought confounds us with its strangeness.
The tractors lie about our fields; at evening
They look like dank sea-monsters couched and waiting.
We leave them where they are and let them rust:
"They'll moulder away and be like other loam".
We make our oxen drag our rusty ploughs,
Long laid aside. We have gone back
Far past our fathers' land.

                  And then, that evening
Late in the summer the strange horses came.
We heard a distant tapping on the road,
A deepening drumming; it stopped, went on again
And at the corner changed to hollow thunder.
We saw the heads
Like a wild wave charging and were afraid.
We had sold our horses in our fathers' time
To buy new tractors. Now they were strange to us
As fabulous steeds set on an ancient shield
Or illustrations in a book of knights.
We did not dare go near them. Yet they waited,
Stubborn and shy, as if they had been sent
By an old command to find our whereabouts
And that long-lost archaic companionship.
In the first moment we had never a thought
That they were creatures to be owned and used.
Among them were some half-a-dozen colts
Dropped in some wilderness of the broken world,
Yet new as if they had come from their own Eden.
Since then they have pulled our ploughs and borne our loads,
But that free servitude still can pierce our hearts.
Our life is changed; their coming our beginning.

Index of Authors

Index of Artists

Text Acknowledgments

The editor and publishers are grateful for permission to reproduce the following copyright material:

"The Runaway" by Robert Frost, from *The Poetry of Robert Frost* edited by Edward Connery Latham, published by Jonathan Cape Ltd and Holt, Rinehart & Winston Inc., reprinted by permission of the editor, the Estate of Robert Frost and the publishers.

The Red Pony by John Steinbeck, copyright 1937, 1938 by John Steinbeck, © renewed 1965, 1966 by John Steinbeck, published by William Heinemann Ltd, and Viking Penguin Inc., extract reprinted by permission of the publishers and Curtis Brown Ltd.

"The Mare's Head" by Alexei Tolstoy, from *Russian Folk Tales* translated by Evgenia Schimanskaya, published by Routledge & Kegan Paul Ltd, reprinted by permission of the publishers.

"Shetland Pony" and "Kelso Horse Show" by Maurice Lindsay, from his *Collected Poems*, published by Paul Harris Publishing, 1979, reprinted by permission of the author and publishers.

"Horse" by George Mackay Brown, from *Portrait of Orkney*, published by The Hogarth Press, 1981, reprinted by permission of the author and publishers.

Akenfield by Ronald Blythe, published by Allen Lane Ltd, 1969, extract reprinted by permission of the author and publishers.

The Horse in the Furrow by George Ewart Evans, published by Faber & Faber Ltd, extract reprinted by permission of the publishers.

Bent's Fort by David Lavender, published by Doubleday & Co Inc., extract reprinted by permission of the publishers; copyright © 1954 by David Lavender.

"A Horse" by Alan Bold, from *This Fine Day*, published by Borderline Press, 1979, reprinted by permission of the author and publishers.

Travel Light by Naomi Mitchison, published by Faber & Faber Ltd, extract reprinted by permission of the author and publishers.

The Horse and His Boy by C. S. Lewis, published by William Collins Sons & Co Ltd, and Macmillan Inc., extract reprinted by permission of the publishers. Copyright C. S. Lewis 1954.

"Horses" by Dorothy Wellesley, published by Granada Publishing Ltd, extract reprinted by permission of the publishers and the executors of the late Dorothy, Duchess of Wellington.

The Brigadier by John Hislop, published by Martin Secker & Warburg Ltd, extract reprinted by permission of the author and publishers.

A Farewell to Arms by Ernest Hemingway, published by Jonathan Cape Ltd, and Charles Scribner's Sons, extract reprinted by permission of the publishers and the Executors of the Ernest Hemingway Estate; copyright 1929 by Charles Scribner's Sons; copyright renewed 1957 by Ernest Hemingway.

The Finish by Sir Alfred Munnings, published by Pitman Books Ltd, extract reprinted by permission of the publishers.

Illustration Acknowledgments

The illustrations on pp. 45, 79 and 228 are reproduced by gracious permission of Her Majesty The Queen.

129   Museum of Fine Arts, Boston, Arthur Gordon Tompkins Residuary Fund
132   Amon Carter
135   The Missouri Historical Society, St Louis
139   from Lear's *Book of Nonsense*, 1862
141   NGL
142   Glasgow, Seton Murray Thomson Collection
143   MEPL
144   Glasgow, Seton Murray Thomson Collection
146   Tate
147   photo Sotheby, King & Chasemore, Pulborough
149   Glasgow, Seton Murray Thomson Collection
152   The Frick Collection
156   NGL
159   NGL
161   BM, MS Add. 11695, sheet 102v
162   Pennsylvania Academy of the Fine Arts
164   Stiftsbibliothek, St Gallen
165   Topkapi Saray Museum, Istanbul
166   Badisches Landesmuseum, Karlsruhe
169   Wallace
171   NGL
175   Private Collection
177   NGL
179   NGL
181   MMA, The Dillon Fund, 1977
183   Elizabeth Frink
187   Château de Versailles (photo Giraudon)
189   Walker Art Gallery, Liverpool
192   MEPL
194   The Iveagh Bequest, Kenwood
195   The Royal Academy
197   Tate
198   The artist and Waddington Graphics
200   The Mansell Collection
202   Musée du Louvre (photo Giraudon)
205   Szépmüvészeti Múzeum, Budapest
206   Amon Carter
211   BM
213   BL, MS Royal 20B.XX53v
214   Musée Condé, Chantilly (photo Giraudon)
216   The Mansell Collection
217   Tate
218   Wallace
220   Tate
221   NGW, Gift of Edgar William and Bernice Chrysler Garbisch
223   The Mansell Collection
225   Glasgow, Seton Murray Thomson Collection